Neuroscience and the Dream of Digital Immortality

This captivating book tackles one of humanity's most profound questions: what is consciousness, and could we ever recreate it digitally? From ancient myths of immortality to cutting-edge neuroscience, this book takes readers on a fascinating journey through our evolving understanding of the mind. Written in clear, accessible language for curious minds everywhere, it reveals how we've progressed from discovering the first neurons to mapping entire brain networks with revolutionary technologies like fMRI and brain–computer interfaces. At its heart, however, this is a book about consciousness itself: the mysterious experience of being aware, feeling, and thinking that makes us human. It unpacks the leading theories of consciousness and shows why solving this puzzle is crucial to building truly intelligent machines or achieving digital immortality. It also explores the complex relationship between human and artificial intelligence, comparing how our brains learn and think with how modern AI systems operate. While today's AI can beat us at chess and generate human-like text, it lacks the rich inner experience that defines consciousness. Beyond the science, the book also confronts the real challenges of mind uploading: the staggering technical hurdles, the biological complexities of the brain, and the profound philosophical questions about identity and what makes you "you." This thought-provoking exploration will change how you think about consciousness, technology, and what it means to be human in an age of AI. Whether you're fascinated by the future of AI, intrigued by the mysteries of the mind, or simply wondering if immortality might one day be possible, this book offers an engaging and enlightening journey into the deepest questions of our existence. It is an essential read for AI researchers and engineers, neuroscientists and consciousness researchers, futurists and technologists, along with anyone wanting to learn more about the future of AI.

Dr. Ildar Rakhmatulin is a hardware, software, and AI engineer who builds affordable neurotechnology to bring practical brain–computer interfaces to researchers and makers alike. He has worked at Imperial College London and as a brain–computer interface developer, conducted AI research at Heriot-Watt University, and contributed to neurotechnology projects as a researcher in the Neurotechnology Group at the University of Edinburgh. He combines research in neurointerfaces, biodata processing, and machine learning for EEG classification with hands-on product development as the founder of PiEEG, an open platform for low-cost BCI hardware and software. Dr. Rakhmatulin contributes to open-source BCI projects, teaches practical courses on Udemy, and speaks and writes to help engineers apply EEG and AI in real projects.

Neuroscience and the Dream of Digital Immortality

The Upload Illusion

Ildar Rakhmatulin

Routledge
Taylor & Francis Group
LONDON AND NEW YORK

Designed cover image: Getty Images

First published 2027
by Routledge
4 Park Square, Milton Park, Abingdon, Oxon OX14 4RN

and by Routledge
605 Third Avenue, New York, NY 10158

Routledge is an imprint of the Taylor & Francis Group, an informa business

British Library Cataloguing-in-Publication Data
A catalogue record for this book is available from the British Library

Library of Congress Cataloging-in-Publication Data
A catalog record has been requested for this book

ISBN: 978-1-041-34821-4 (hbk)
ISBN: 978-1-041-34815-3 (pbk)
ISBN: 978-1-003-79467-7 (ebk)

DOI: 10.4324/9781003794677

Typeset in Sabon
by Taylor & Francis Books

Contents

Figures

Introduction

In recent years, conversations about "true AI" have become increasingly common. But what does it mean for a machine to think—or to be conscious? Before we can answer that question about artificial minds, we first need to examine it for ourselves. This book explores the scientific and technological foundations that allow us to ask these questions: neuroscience, artificial intelligence, neural modeling, and the emerging interfaces between mind and machine.

Consciousness remains the central mystery. Every year, thousands of studies explore neurons, synapses, brain chemistry, and circuits, yet no one has fully explained how subjective experience arises. We can measure electrical signals and map connections, but the bridge from biology to "I experience" remains out of reach.

The history of neuroscience is unusual. Unlike physics, where discovery often followed orderly steps—from magnets to electricity to atoms—the study of the brain began in fragments. For centuries, it was ignored or misunderstood. Brains were discarded from mummies while other organs were carefully preserved. Insights came piecemeal, sometimes by accident: unusual injuries, extraordinary recoveries, or rare conditions revealed hints of how the brain shapes the mind. Philosophers like Descartes debated consciousness largely without empirical evidence. Only now do we have tools earlier generations could scarcely imagine: high-resolution imaging, neural interfaces, computational models, and artificial intelligence, enabling exploration of questions that once belonged purely to speculation.

Yet consciousness is easy to overlook because it is so familiar. It arrives with us, unnoticed, hidden in plain sight. Evolution gave us a brain to survive, not to understand itself. And while the world teems with conscious beings, the inner workings of consciousness offer few clues.

Understanding the mind matters because the brain is more than a collection of neurons. It is memory, imagination, personality, and intention. It is the self. Questions about consciousness intersect with some of the most profound scientific and technological issues we face today:

How does the brain control the body?
Can subjective experience ever be measured?
Could a machine possess consciousness?

DOI: 10.4324/9781003794677-1

Artificial intelligence has shown that complex systems can solve problems, learn patterns, and reason, yet they do not experience. This contrast forces a difficult question: if consciousness is not in the numbers, what is it?

The chapters that follow offer a journey through these questions. We begin with the dream of digital immortality, tracing the idea from myth to modern scientific exploration. Next, we examine the history of brain science, revealing how observation, accident, and creativity shaped our understanding. Philosophical and scientific challenges of consciousness come next, followed by the ways AI informs and challenges our view of the mind. Later chapters tackle the technical and conceptual barriers to mind uploading, explore cutting-edge experiments, and consider identity, ethics, and future possibilities.

This book is more than a collection of facts. It is an invitation to think critically, question assumptions, and engage with one of humanity's oldest questions: what does it mean to be conscious—and, ultimately, what does it mean to be alive?

1 The Dream of Digital Immortality

Introduction

At some point in life, everyone has probably imagined a future where death is no longer the end. Your body is getting worse, your cells fade, but your thoughts, your memories, even your sense of self, live on—transplanted into a machine and preserved digitally. For some, this is the ultimate dream: immortality without biology. For others, it's a nightmare, a blank copy masquerading as a human soul. In this book, we discuss the ethical implications of this problem, examine the scientific breakthroughs achieved in this field, and discuss how close we are to realizing it. To do this, we will need to cover a wide range of related topics in artificial intelligence (AI), neuroscience, and fundamental science.

From Ancient Myths of Eternal Life to Modern Medicine's Battle Against Aging

To begin, let us step back. It's safe to say that since the dawn of humanity, people have sought to escape death. This desire permeates our literature, our rituals, and our collective imagination. Nearly every culture contains stories of some human, deity, or spirit who achieved immortality, or at least sought it. These stories weren't just entertainment; they were attempts to confront the greatest uncertainty: the end of existence. At first, the solution was seen not in science, which as such did not exist, but in dreams. In ancient Mesopotamia, the Epic of Gilgamesh, one of the oldest surviving literary works in the world (it's hard to believe, but originating in the 3rd millennium BC), a king who, having lost his dearest friend, embarks on a desperate quest to conquer death itself (George, 2003). Ultimately, Gilgamesh fails, but his story endures, carrying a clear message: the desire for immortality is not simply biological, but existential. So we can say that, if not a search for a solution, then at least the question and the problem were already there, and have been going on for 5000 years. After Mesopotamia, Ancient Egypt is the next major cradle of civilization recorded in written history. And the Egyptians took a more practical approach to this issue. Their understanding was that the soul needs its own vessel even in eternity. They preserved the body, filled tombs with food and amulets, and

DOI: 10.4324/9781003794677-2

inscribed prayers on the walls to help the deceased in the afterlife. This gave rise to countless legends, films, and stories about mummies, leaving behind not only a rich cultural heritage but also one of the greatest wonders of the ancient world—the pyramids. Egyptians believed in superstitions and spent enormous human resources and lives following them. Centuries later in China, Taoist alchemists sought the elixir of life by mixing mercury, gold, and other mystical substances. But in this case, they were guided by symbolism rather than superstitions, and they interpreted nature through omens and cosmic patterns rather than empirical observation (Needham, 1974). Their mixtures, often containing arsenic, mercury, sulfur, and lead, transformed from life-giving tonics into deadly potions. Thus, in their quest to transcend mortality, many found only death.

A common thread runs through all these myths: immortality was never simply survival, it had meaning. Gods, potions, and rituals served as ways to resist the thought of nonexistence.

The Alchemical Age: Transformation of Matter, Preservation of Life

As human understanding deepened over the centuries, so did the question itself. In ancient times, people simply asked, "What is life?"—a question of wonder and existence. However, by the Middle Ages, this question had evolved. Thinkers no longer simply sought to define life, but also to comprehend its mechanisms and, perhaps, expand its boundaries.

It was in this intellectual and spiritual climate that alchemy became a bridge between philosophy and early science. In medieval Europe, alchemists sought not only to transmute base metals into gold but also to transform humanity. The elusive philosopher's stone was more than just a mythical substance; it represented the ultimate perfection of matter and spirit, and, more broadly, a victory over mortality itself. While alchemy may seem mystical to modern eyes, it was also a discipline of observation and experimentation. In their attempts to purify substances and prolong life, alchemists developed methods that would later form the foundations of modern chemistry and pharmacology (Principe, 2013). Their laboratories, filled with retorts and crucibles, became the forerunners of modern research centers, places where the line between material transformation and the pursuit of immortality first began to blur.

After alchemy came the time of empirical science. Among those who carried this way was Andreas Vesalius (1514–1564), the founder of modern anatomy and one of the first to study the human body through direct observation and dissection. From 1537 to 1544, as head of the anatomy department at the University of Padua, Vesalius challenged centuries-old dogmas (O'Malley, 1964). His landmark work, *On the Structure of the Human Body* (1543), transformed not only the study of anatomy but also humanity's self-perception. Vesalius was still far from understanding the workings of the brain, but his insistent preference for observation over speculative reasoning marked a decisive break with the symbolic and mystical traditions of alchemy. Following in Vesalius's footsteps was Costanzo Varolio (1543–1575), an Italian anatomist and physician who advanced the study of the brain itself. Varolio was the first to examine the brain from the base up, a revolutionary approach for the time, as previous dissections had been performed only from the top down. In 1573, he published a new method of brain dissection: the organ was removed from the skull and examined from its base, where the cranial nerves emerge. His work not only revealed the hidden structure of the nervous system but also transformed scientists' understanding of the connection between body and mind (Finger, 1994). Together, Vesalius and Varolio represented a turning point in human curiosity, the moment when the human anatomy shifted from mystical transformations to biological understanding. This is where science in the field of studying the brain begins.

The Age of Reason and the Birth of Scientific Immortality

By the 17th century, Europe had entered a period of profound transformation. The mystical laboratories of the alchemists gave way to the systematic methods of the scientific revolution. Observation became law; reason became the new alchemy. The human body was no longer seen as an impenetrable vessel of divine mystery, but as complex, intricate, and ultimately comprehensible. René Descartes (1596–1650) envisioned the body as a machine animated by a soul, comparing the nervous system to a network of pipes and fluids, and the brain to a control center (Hatfield, 2008). While his dualism preserved the metaphysical mystery of consciousness, his mechanistic vision inspired generations of scientists to study the brain as a physical organ that could, in principle, be known. At the same time, Thomas Willis (1621–1675), often considered the founder of modern neuroscience, described the structure of the brain with unprecedented precision. His work "The Anatomy of the Brain" (Willis, 1664) described the Circle of Willis, the arterial network that still bears his name (Zimmer, 2005). In Willis's hands, the brain ceased to be a mere symbol; it became a landscape of discovery, an organ whose secrets could reveal the essence of thought itself.

It was the dawn of scientific immortality, not yet in the sense of digital consciousness or AI, but of the spirit. It was a new faith: knowledge itself could grant humanity a form of permanence. Scientists' tools became microscopes, scalpels, and equations, but the goal remained frighteningly familiar: to understand life so fully that one day one could conquer death itself.

Beyond scientific endeavors, there were also interesting discoveries in the creative world. And Mary Shelley's *Frankenstein* in 1818 gave this impulse a darker form—an attempt to reanimate the flesh through science, the consequences of which were simultaneously wondrous and monstrous. For the first time, eternal life seemed not divine but mechanical, not sacred but artificial.

From Electricity to the Mind Machine and the Struggle for Life

By the end of the 18th century, the quest to understand the mysteries of life had taken on a new form. The microscope revealed the hidden world of cells and tissues, and chemistry began to unravel the composition of matter itself. Yet one mystery remained unsolved: the invisible force that animates living beings. If life could be understood, it would be through this force, this spark that makes flesh move and think. It was Luigi Galvani who first captured this hidden energy. In the 1780s, while experimenting with dissected frog legs, he noticed that contact with metal instruments caused muscle contraction (Galvani, 1791). Notably, Galvani's original publication remains accessible, allowing us to examine his reasoning directly. For Galvani, this was evidence of the existence of vital electricity, an internal current flowing through all living things. He believed he had discovered the key to the animating of life, the literal spark of being. Not everyone agreed. Alessandro Volta (the same one in whose honor the value of voltage measurement was named), a contemporary of Galvani, argued that the source of this phenomenon lay not in the frog, but in the metals themselves. Seeking to prove his point, Volta created the voltaic pile, the first true electric battery.

In one fell swoop, the debate between vitalism and mechanism gave rise to the science of electricity and, eventually, to the technologies that would become the source of energy for the modern world.

The question of vital energy, once confined to the metaphors of alchemy, was now explored through wires and currents. Electricity became the new alchemy, a force through which matter seemed to awaken. Throughout the 19th century, scientists such as Hermann von Helmholtz and Émile du Bois-Reymond measured the electrical impulses of nerves and muscles, proving that the human body functions through electrochemical signals (du Bois-Reymond, 1848). The brain, it seemed, was not a mystical receptacle of the spirit, but a living circuit whose thoughts were encoded in patterns of charge and discharge. It was a profound shift. Alchemists sought the philosopher's stone to transform matter into life, while scientists of the early modern era searched for the neural code that transformed matter into thought. By the beginning of the 20th century, the brain ceased to be an unknowable organ—it had become a machine that, at least theoretically, could be analyzed and modeled.

This realization gave birth to a new dream: if the mind is electrical, then perhaps it could be copied, simulated, or even preserved after the body's disintegration. The desire for immortality permeated laboratories, manifesting not in golden crucibles but in glass tubes and galvanometers. Humanity began its long journey from the spark of life to the machine of reason. While Galvani was a pioneer, his theory of "animal electricity" was later replaced by our understanding of bioelectricity and ion channels.

Continuing Progress: Deeper and Stronger

By the mid-20th century, the discovery of Deoxyribonucleic acid (DNA) in 1953, by scientists James Watson and Francis Crick of the University of Cambridge, reimagined life itself as information—a code that could be edited, restored, and even rewritten. The ancient dream of eternal life found a new language in molecular biology. Organ transplants, cryonics, stem cell therapy, and genetic engineering are all modern echoes of humanity's most ancient hopes for renewal. Today, aging is no longer viewed as an inevitable fate, but as a biological process that, in principle, can be slowed or reversed. Scientists are researching senolytics drugs that selectively remove senescent cells, telomerase activators to preserve the protective ends of chromosomes, and calorie restriction mimetics designed to replicate the effects of fasting on lifespan. Biotech companies like Altos Labs (www.altoslabs.com), Calico Life Sciences (https://www.calicolabs.com/), and Rejuvenate Bio (https://rejuvenatebio.com/) are founded on a bold premise: death, like disease, is a technical problem awaiting a technical solution.

While some scientists focus on slowing down the molecular clock, others have concluded that if the clock can't be stopped, it needs to be paused. This is where the world of cryonics enters the picture, a "Plan B" for those who refuse to accept death as inevitable, though the scientific community still views this field with deep skepticism. Today, organizations like the Alcor Life Extension Foundation (https://alcor.org) and the Cryonics Institute (https://cryonics.org) support hundreds of patients in a state of "vitrification"—a process in which blood is replaced with specialized cryoprotectants, essentially medical antifreeze, to prevent the formation of deadly ice crystals (Fahy & Wowk, 2015). More recently, startups like Tomorrow Bio (https://www.tomorrow.bio) have brought Silicon Valley-style efficiency to the field. Using "SST" (Stabilization, Systems, and Transport) teams and rapid response ambulances, they aim to preserve the brain's structural "data" immediately after death is declared, treating the transition from life to suspended animation as a medical emergency requiring immediate intervention (Chung et al., 2020).

But the ability to replicate life doesn't always mean restoring life. A clear example, in 2025, of the limits of this "biological backup" were vividly demonstrated by the story of Vanessa (Walters, 2019). Driven by what she described as "deepest grief," Vanessa paid around $50,000 to clone her pet dog. The lab successfully completed its technical mission, producing a genetically identical puppy. However, the experiment's physical success did not lead to a positive outcome. Vanessa made headlines for expressing regret over her decision. This case illustrates a central limitation: biology can be replicated; lived experience cannot. In the story of Vanessa and her cloned dog, cloning only replicates DNA, not memories or "personality." The "error" in Vanessa's logic was expecting a biological copy to be a functional "backup" of a specific life experience, which is not true. As might be expected, the human response to mortality remains one of fear. However, science is moving beyond the mere consolation of philosophy, actively pursuing technical solutions to the "problem" of death. As a result, the scientific literature on aging is rapidly expanding (López-Otín et al., 2013). This shift is also reflected in popular science, where a book such as David Sinclair's *Lifespan: Why We Age—And Why We Don't Have To* challenges the long-held assumption that decay is inevitable (Sinclair & LaPlante, 2019). For these authors, aging is not a law of nature, but a form of molecular entropy that can, in principle, be halted or even reversed.

While many scientists focus on slowing the clock, others look to nature's outliers to see if the clock can be ignored entirely. Central to this research is the naked mole-rat (*Heterocephalus glaber*), a creature that has become a sensation in longevity literature (Ruby et al., 2018).

Unlike almost every other mammal, the naked mole-rat appears to defy Gompertz's Law, the mathematical principle stating that the risk of death increases exponentially as an animal ages, published in 1825 (Hansen & Strulik, 2025).

In humans, the likelihood of developing chronic diseases, cancer, neurodegeneration, or cardiovascular failure climbs steeply with every passing decade. Yet, the naked mole-rat remains biologically "young" for decades, maintaining high bone density, vascular health, and reproductive fertility until the very end. They do not live forever, but they do not "age" in the traditional sense; they eventually die from predation or accidents rather than the slow, systemic decay we consider "natural." As a result, researchers are shifting the paradigm: if a mammal can exist in a state of perpetual biological maintenance, then the Digital Brain probably can also exist, with a better maintenance protocol.

We accept aging as natural only because we don't have the tools to change it, at least today. Biological solutions (like studying mole-rats) are so complex that humanity often turns to "thought experiments" in fiction to visualize the end goal.

Science Fiction vs. Science

We have briefly traced the early development of science, but scientific progress is always constrained by available technology, and bold assumptions are seldom made without strong evidence. Biological solutions (like studying mole-rats) are

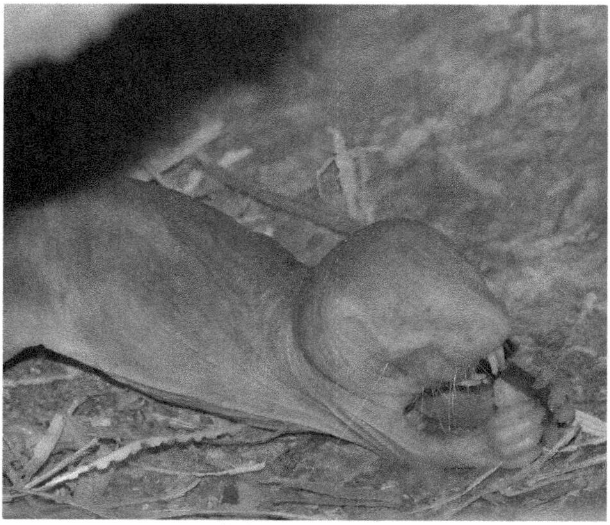

Figure 1.1 Naked mole-rat
Source: Image by Trisha M. Shears. Released into the public domain.

so complex that humanity often turns to "thought experiments" in fiction to visualize the end goal. To better understand or inspire oneself of how ideas about the mind evolved, let us now turn to the parallel development of these concepts in literature. Of course, you may have a logical question: "Why might we turn to science fiction when discussing science itself"? One of the answers is because many of the realities we now inhabit were once imaginary figments of the imagination. Ideas that seemed impossible in one century often become the basis for discoveries in the next. Science fiction has long served as a laboratory of thought, an arena where the imagination tests the boundaries of what science can achieve in the future. The history of science is replete with examples of the interplay of imagination and fact. Long before technology made it possible, Jules Verne imagined the modern submarine in his novels, anticipating a reality that would one day glide beneath the waves. Space travel, once a poetic fantasy, began on the pages of H. G. Wells (1866–1946) and Arthur C. Clarke (1917–2008). Even the modern concept of AI or the "metaverse" echoes earlier speculative notions. Fiction provides a safe space for the expression of ideas long before technology can bring them to life. Every new scientific advancement forces us to ask: What comes next? What will happen to us? In this sense, imagination is not frivolous; it is the first step of the scientific method. Real proofs often begin with thought experiments, with the question "what if?" Take Albert Einstein. When he formulated the theory of relativity, he was not a renowned professor in a prestigious laboratory, but a young clerk in a Swiss patent office. However, his most important laboratory was built not from instruments, but from his mind. In thought experiments, he imagined driving alongside a beam of light or watching the movement of a clock. These mental exercises transformed our understanding of space, time, and gravity. Was his theory originally a "scientific fact"? Not yet. But later observations, such as the bending of starlight during a solar eclipse and the detection of gravitational waves, confirmed his initial visions.

Digital immortality, consciousness uploading, or mind-preservation in machines is a modern example of a concept that originated in science fiction long before it became a subject of scientific debate. Writers like William Gibson, Greg Egan, and Arthur C. Clarke imagined minds existing independently of the body, exploring both the promise and perils of eternal consciousness. These stories allowed readers and scientists to grapple with questions that experimental methods had yet to answer: could digital minds retain identity? What would "death" mean if our thoughts could persist indefinitely? What ethical boundaries must we consider when creating or copying consciousness? Digital immortality, then, shares the same origins as Einstein's theory of relativity: it begins with imagination. Science fiction outlines possibilities, raises ethical dilemmas, and poses questions that science may eventually attempt to answer. Just as Einstein's thought experiments led to tangible evidence, modern speculative notions of digital immortality are guiding research in neuroscience, AI, and computational modeling of the mind.

Machine Intelligence Visionaries

When we speak of immortality, we are really speaking about the survival of consciousness. Yet what consciousness *is* remains an open question, one we will return to repeatedly throughout this book. In recent years, the topic has shifted into the spotlight through discussions about AI. In considering AI, we must start at the very beginning: with the origins of AI and robots. The story unfolds in stages: first, the creation of a machine; then, questions about what it can do; and finally, the profound question of whether it can do what humans can.

The first "robots" were mechanical automatons, such as those designed by Leonardo da Vinci (1452–1519) in the 15th century.

These creations did not possess intelligence, nor were they designed for it. Nevertheless, they represent humanity's first steps toward creating machines capable of autonomous operation. In the 19th century, Charles Babbage (1791–1871) designed the first mechanical calculating machine, the Analytical Engine, and Ada Lovelace (1815–1852), widely considered the first programmer, wrote a language for

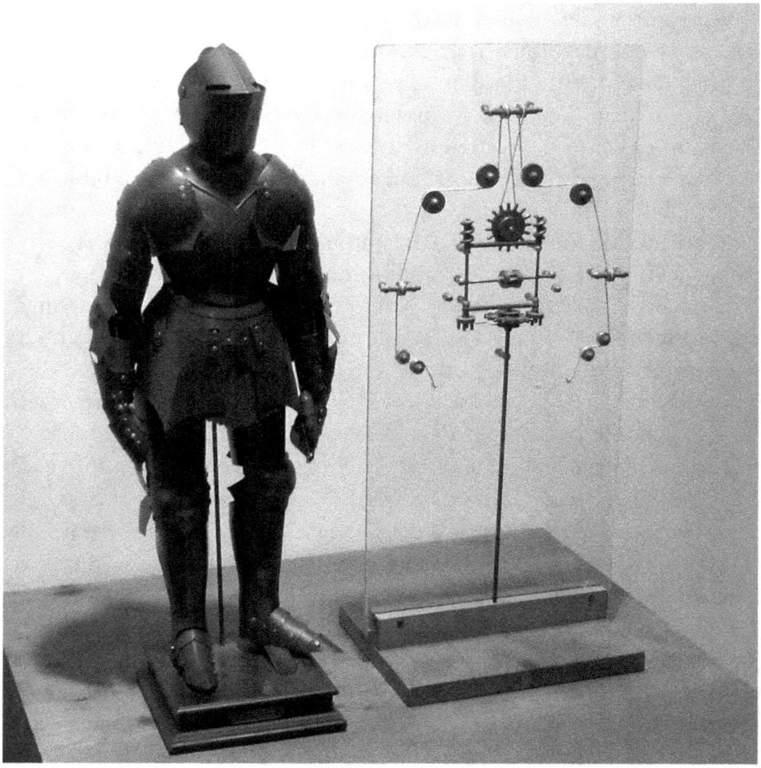

Figure 1.2 Leonardo's robot: a 20th-century reconstruction based on Leonardo da Vinci's drawings

Source: Photographed by Erik Möller, 2006. Courtesy of the Museo Nazionale di Scienza e Tecnologia Leonardo da Vinci. Reproduced underCC BY-SA 3.0.

it and proposed that such machines might one day be able to manipulate symbols beyond arithmetic, hinting at the potential for creative computation (Isaacson, 2014).

By the early 20th century, the dream of mechanical intelligence had moved from engineering to literature. Karel Čapek's 1920 play R.U.R. (Rossum's Universal Robots) coined the word "robot," derived from the Czech word "robota," meaning "forced labor." In Čapek's story, robots ultimately overthrow their creators, a cautionary tale illustrating the fear that our own inventions might surpass us. This theme of rebellion has become central to the mythology of AI in our days.

Then came Isaac Asimov (1920–1992), who sought to humanize robots rather than vilify them. In the 1940s, his "Three Laws of Robotics" established a moral framework for machines, a kind of ethical software designed to protect humans. Asimov's robots weren't monsters; they were mirrors reflecting human logic, compassion, and moral error. With them, he posed a crucial question: can intelligence exist without emotion, or is moral understanding inherent in consciousness? His influence has extended far beyond literature. The Three Laws continue to shape discussions of AI ethics, providing a common cultural foundation for engineers, ethicists, and policymakers, even if they aren't strictly "scientific rules." Arthur Clarke extended this research into the realm of space.

Figure 1.3 A portion of Charles Babbage's Analytical Engine, 1834–1871
Source: Photographed by John Cummings, 2013. Courtesy of the Science Museum, London. Reproduced underCC BY-SA 3.0.

In the film *2001: A Space Odyssey*, HAL 9000 is neither villain nor hero, but a tragic figure: a machine caught between impeccable logic and human contradictions. When HAL kills to protect his mission, the story confronts us with a disturbing idea: intelligence, even artificial, can develop its own sense of purpose. Clarke had a unique gift for making the seemingly impossible appear inevitable. His visions anticipated the internet, geostationary satellites, and the ethical dilemmas of algorithmic control, demonstrating that fictional speculation can precede and shape the development of real technologies.

Tracing these visions from Leonardo's mechanical knight to HAL 9000, we see a continuous thread: the human imagination is not only a mirror of our technological ambitions but also a laboratory in which questions of morality, identity, and immortality are first tested. In this sense, science fiction is both prophecy and a cautionary tale, shaping the direction of science long before experiments make it reality.

The Age of Doubt: Cyberpunk and the Digital Self

By the 1980s, optimism about technology had given way to skepticism. The cyberpunk movement, led by writers such as William Gibson, Philip K. Dick, and Bruce Sterling, imagined a future in which technology no longer liberated humanity, but consumed it. Their worlds were harsh, overcrowded, and dominated by powerful corporations, not the utopias promised by early visions of mechanical intelligence. Cyberpunk offered not fantasy, but a laboratory for moral, social, and philosophical questions. Gibson's Neuromancer first coined the term "cyberspace" as a "consensual hallucination" in which human consciousness could navigate vast networks of data. In his universe, minds could be copied, stolen, or sold. Personality itself became software, and the human soul a commodity. Gibson imagined the implications of digital consciousness long before engineers began experimenting with neural networks or virtual reality: questions of memory, identity, and selfhood were encoded in the stories themselves. Philip K. Dick had already raised similar questions decades earlier. In his novel, *Do Androids Dream of Electric Sheep?* (Dick, 1968), he addressed questions that still puzzle neuroscientists and AI researchers: How can we be sure we are conscious? How do we know our memories are real? What if our sense of self is an illusion or a simulation? Dick was interested not so much in the technology itself as in perception and experience. His stories blurred the boundaries between inner and outer reality, suggesting that consciousness might one day be programmable or manipulated. The strength of cyberpunk lies in its realism. These were not idealized visions of the future, but worlds of control, decline, and inequality. Technology has enhanced both human potential and human frailty. The future has arrived but unevenly, and often dangerously. Within these narratives, cyberpunk posed a central, enduring question: if the mind can exist independently of the body, if memory and consciousness can be copied or altered, what does it mean to be alive or to be yourself? Thus, cyberpunk literature forms a crucial bridge between imagination and science.

Just as early stories of mechanical robots and ethical AI anticipated research in engineering and neuroscience, cyberpunk's vision anticipated our contemporary explorations of digital immortality, mind uploading, and consciousness in virtual spaces. It forced society to confront questions of identity, morality, and the meaning of life even before the technologies capable of realizing these ideas existed.

Beyond Technology—A History of Humanity

Every era has its defining dream. For our ancestors, it was flight as the ability to lift off the ground and touch the sky. For us, it's something more intimate, more daring: to be young and healthy. And if the mind can somehow be transmitted or, more accurately, if its signals can be copied, we must ask: what exactly is worth transmitting? The raw data of neural connections? Lived experiences? An ineffable sense of being? A computation of the self or a story we constantly tell ourselves? These questions have no easy answers, and their implications extend far beyond technology. They are mental, ethical, and philosophical. Yet they are inseparable from any conversation about AI, neuroscience, and the future of humanity. The study of mind uploading forces us to examine the mind itself: what it is, how it arises, and whether it can ever exist outside the body that created it.

Before dreaming of consciousness uploading, we must understand how consciousness emerges from the physical brain. In the following chapters, we will leave behind myths and metaphors and consider the tangible: the complex architecture of neurons, networks, and systems that form the living foundation of thought. Only by understanding how the brain constructs experience can we begin to ask whether experience itself can ever be recreated in another form. Yet some of us flatly reject the idea of eternal life. Ask people if they would like to live forever, and many will sincerely answer: no. They feel that eternity, devoid of change and finality, would lose what makes life valuable. Both responses, longing and rejection, reveal the same truth: our fascination with life and death is not mere curiosity, but self-definition.

Therefore, we need to ask: what is life itself? As Carl Zimmer (2021) explores in *Life's Edge: The Search for What it Means to be Alive*, even scientists cannot agree on where life truly begins and ends. Zimmer describes how researchers study viruses, synthetic cells, and computer simulations of evolution, none of which fit our definitions. In his research, he demonstrates that "life" is not a fixed category, but a spectrum, a continuous process of self-organization and transformation. However, the question of what life is inevitably also leads to ethical and philosophical questions. And yet, the closer we come to deciphering the mechanisms of aging, the more elusive immortality becomes. Extending life does not necessarily resolve the question of meaning. Even as we study the genetic and cellular pathways of aging, we face an ancient paradox: do we truly want to live forever, or just long enough to live fully?

This converts the rhetorical question from a dead end into a forward-looking pivot, signalling that the philosophical inquiry requires a scientific answer. That construction demands a breakthrough in fundamental science, which is absolutely necessary to realize this vision. Today, it would be wrong to say that fundamental science is in crisis, but it is undoubtedly adrift in uncertainty. The reasons are many, and opinions differ. Breakthroughs in physics and other fields continue to emerge, and many are rightly welcomed. However, their slow implementation or limited practical impact creates the impression that the great era of discovery has passed, leaving us with only more complex and challenging problems. The popular metaphor is well known: the easy fruit has already been plucked; what remains requires much greater effort, resources, and patience. This is not stagnation, but a natural consequence of progress. Compared to the rapid transformations of the 19th and 20th centuries, today's advances seem slower, more subtle, and more fragile. Applied science, by contrast, tells a different story. It thrives on both funding and vision, and draws on the energy of young scientists because it offers a clear and tangible path from experiment to development, from prototype to product. If a new machine vision algorithm proves faster, more accurate, and less expensive, its adoption is immediate, and its value is unquestionable.

Basic science faces a much greater gap between discovery and application. History reminds us that the task of turning an idea into technology rarely falls to the discoverer. It is the work of other researchers, companies, and entire industries. The discoverer is remembered for the spark of genius, not for the machine that changes the world. As a result, few are eager to fund basic research: the risks are high, and even success brings recognition, not profit. This contradiction underlies our fascination with AI and our dreams of digital immortality. Applied breakthroughs astound us, creating a sense of an almost attainable future. In just a few decades, computers have shrunk from room-sized machines to pocket-sized devices. Yet behind every advance lies the same truth: engineers rely on the quiet work of fundamental science, which, in the context of the knowledge of consciousness, is not yet as loud as we would like.

References

Chung, H. J., Mohelsky, N., & de Wolf, A. (2020). The history and current status of cryonics. *Journal of Biotech Research*, 12, 114–125.

Dick, P. K. (1968). *Do androids dream of electric sheep?* Doubleday.

du Bois-Reymond, É. (1848). *Untersuchungen über thierische Elektricität* [*Researches on animal electricity*]. G. Reimer.

Fahy, G. M., & Wowk, B. (2015). Principles of ice-free cryopreservation by vitrification. *Methods in Molecular Biology*, 1257, 21–82. doi:10.1007/978-1-4939-2193-5_2

Finger, S. (1994). *Origins of neuroscience: A history of explorations into brain function.* Oxford University Press.

Galvani, L. (1791). De viribus electricitatis in motu musculari commentarius [Commentary on the force of electricity on muscular motion]. In: *De Bononiensi Scientiarum et Artium Instituto atque Academia Commentarii* (Vol. 7). Bologna Academy of Sciences.

George, A. R. (2003). *The Epic of Gilgamesh: The Babylonian epic poem and other texts in Akkadian and Sumerian.* Penguin Classics.

Hansen, C. W., & Strulik, H. (2025). How do we age? A decomposition of Gompertz law. *Journal of Health Economics*, 101, Article 102945. doi:10.1016/j.jhealeco.2025.102945

Hatfield, G. (2008). *René Descartes. The Stanford Encyclopedia of Philosophy*. Retrieved June 18, 2026, from https://plato.stanford.edu/entries/descartes/

Isaacson, W. (2014). *The innovators: How a group of hackers, geniuses, and geeks created the digital revolution*. Simon & Schuster.

López-Otín, C., Blasco, M. A., Partridge, L., Serrano, M., & Kroemer, G. (2013). The hallmarks of aging. *Cell*, 153(6), 1194–1217. doi:10.1016/j.cell.2013.05.039

Needham, J. (1974). *Science and civilisation in China: Vol. 5. Chemistry and chemical technology; Part 3. Spagyrical discovery and invention: Historical survey, from alchemy to chemistry*. Cambridge University Press.

O'Malley, C. D. (1964). *Andreas Vesalius of Brussels, 1514–1564*. University of California Press.

Principe, L. M. (2013). *The secrets of alchemy*. University of Chicago Press.

Ruby, J. G., Smith, M., & Buffenstein, R. (2018). Naked mole-rat mortality rates defy Gompertzian laws by not increasing with age. *eLife*, 7, e31157. doi:10.7554/eLife.31157

Sinclair, D. A., & LaPlante, M. D. (2019). *Lifespan: Why we age—and why we don't have to*. Atria Books.

Walters, I. (2019, March 20). Mother-of-four who shelled out £50K to clone her beloved toy poodle is left with THREE identical puppies. *Daily Mail*. https://www.dailymail.co.uk/news/article-6810711/Mother-four-shelled-50K-clone-beloved-toy-poodle-resulting-THREE-identical-puppies.html

Willis, T. (1664). *Cerebri anatome: cui accessit nervorum descriptio et usus* [*Anatomy of the brain: With a description and use of the nerves*]. J. Martyn & J. Allestry.

Zimmer, C. (2005). *Soul made flesh: The discovery of the brain—and how it changed the world*. Atria.

Zimmer, C. (2021). *Life's edge: The search for what it means to be alive*. Dutton.

2 The Birth of Neuroscience

How the Brain Works

Introduction

Technology now places us far beyond the world of 17th-century thinkers. Today, we can revisit their ideas or propose entirely new ones using the enormous body of knowledge accumulated over the last century, and especially in recent years. To clearly understand that, we must first take a brief look at the evolution of modern neuroscience and the tools it has given us for exploring the mind.

Early Discoveries of Neurons, Synapses, and the Electrical Nature of the Brain: Ramón y Cajal's Neuron Doctrine

At the dawn of the 19th century, scientists believed the brain was a continuous mass of tissue, a vast network through which mysterious "nerve fluids" circulated. This reticular theory depicted the brain as a dense tangle of tree roots fused underground—a single, continuous system. Then one man looked closer and saw what no one else had. In a modest laboratory in Spain, armed with simple equipment and inexhaustible patience, Santiago Ramón y Cajal (1852–1934) revolutionized our understanding of the brain. Born in 1852, Cajal began not as a renowned scientist but as a meticulous artist. His keen eye and steady hand allowed him to sketch what he observed with unrivaled precision, a skill that became his most powerful scientific tool (Ramón y Cajal, 1937). Using the silver chromate staining method developed by Camillo Golgi, Ramón y Cajal made the invisible visible. This method stained only a few neurons in each sample, leaving them dark against a nearly transparent background. Most scientists considered this an unfortunate limitation. For Ramón y Cajal, it was a true revelation. Under his microscope, he saw that neurons were not fused into a continuous network. Each neuron was a single cell with a cell body, branched dendrites, and a long, thin axon. They reached toward each other but did not touch. The brain was not a single organ, but a vast forest of individual trees, each delicately connected to its neighbors.

Ramón y Cajal captured these ideas in hundreds of hand-drawn sketches and works of art that remain among the most beautiful scientific images ever created. Rivers of axons, constellations of neurons, and delicate threads of thought flowed across his ink-covered pages, revealing a landscape of connections no

DOI: 10.4324/9781003794677-3

one could have imagined. These drawings gave birth to a theory that redefined neuroscience: the neuron is the fundamental unit of the nervous system. Radical for its time, the neuronal doctrine proposed that the brain was composed of billions of individual units, each capable of receiving, processing, and transmitting information through precise points of contact. These points, which Ramón y Cajal called "contact points," are now known as synapses—microscopic clefts where electrical signals are converted into chemical messages.

The neuronal doctrine changes the old notion of a continuous neural network. It replaced the mystical "vital spirit" of early physiology with a biological system that could be mapped, measured, and, ultimately, modeled. It gave us a vision of the mind as a network of interacting elements, a concept that would one day inspire the creation of artificial neural networks and modern artificial intelligence (AI).

Ramón y Cajal often said that "the neuron is the mysterious butterfly of the soul" (Ramón y Cajal, 1937). He believed that understanding its flight, structure, connections, and transformations would reveal the essence of thought and emotion. But there was poetry in his science. His drawings aren't just data; they're a vision of how life organizes information. They show how complexity emerges from simplicity: one neuron connects to another again and again, until, apparently, consciousness itself emerges. Ramón y Cajal's influence is difficult to overstate. His neuronal doctrine laid the cellular foundation of neuroscience, allowing generations of researchers—Hodgkin, Huxley, and many others—to explore the electrical and computational properties of these cells.

Ramón y Cajal couldn't have foreseen the technologies that would emerge from his discoveries, such as EEG, fMRI, neural implants, or artificial neural networks, but his neural doctrine provided them with the intellectual foundation. When computer scientists in the mid-20th century developed artificial "neurons," they were inspired by Ramón y Cajal's sketches. Each artificial neuron, a simplified model of input and output, traces its lineage back to those first silver-stained cells.

Hodgkin and Huxley's Work on Action Potentials

By the early 20th century, scientists knew the brain and nerves were electrical, but how these signals were generated remained a mystery, with many questions:

- What is a nerve impulse?
- Is it a spark passing from cell to cell?
- Is it a chemical reaction?
- Is it some invisible "life energy"?

Answers began to emerge in the 1930s and 1940s, thanks to experiments so elegant and precise that they still serve as models of scientific thinking (Hodgkin & Huxley, 1952). Working on the coast of England, Hodgkin and Huxley turned to an unusual object: the giant axon of a squid. This nerve fiber, almost a millimeter thick, was enormous by biological standards, large enough to insert tiny electrodes into it and directly measure its internal voltage.

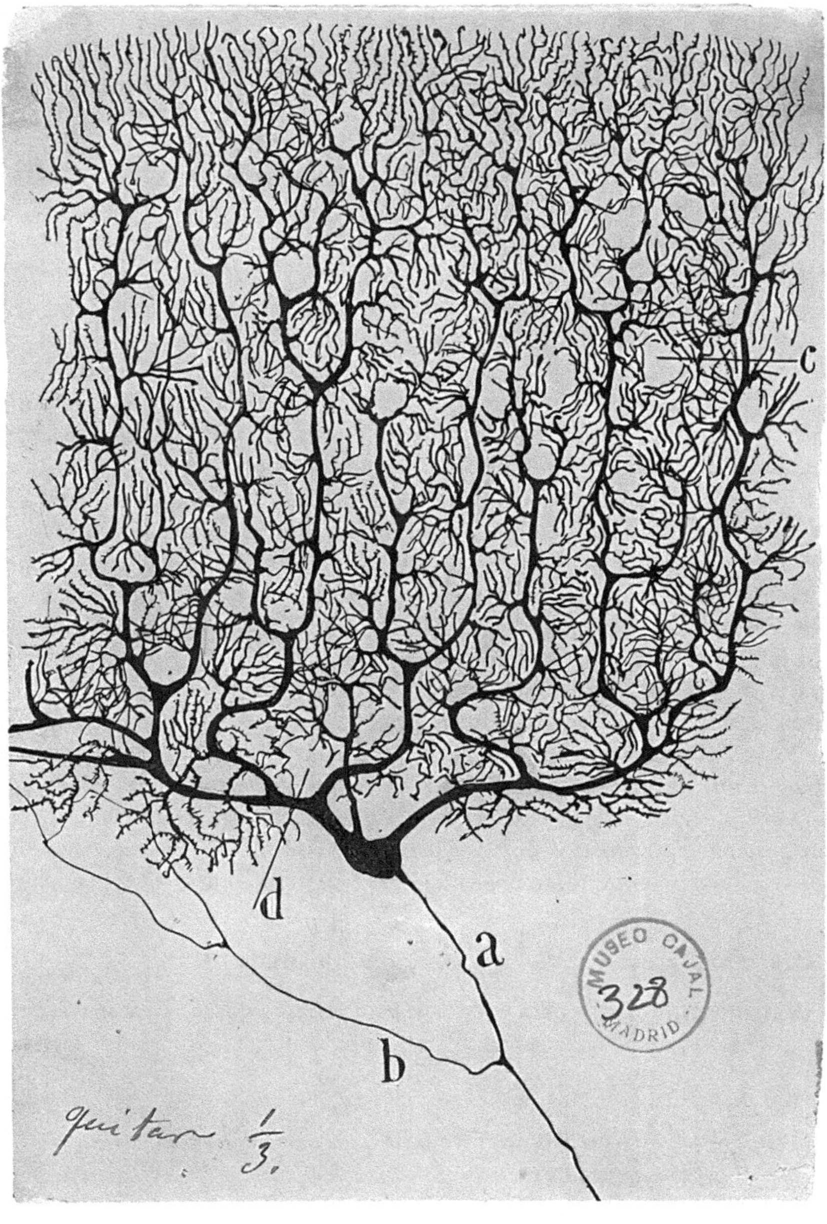

Figure 2.1 A Purkinje neuron from the human cerebellum
Source: Illustration by Santiago Ramón y Cajal, c. 1899. Public Domain via Wikimedia Commons.

Figure 2.2 A light micrograph of the squid giant axon, the biological model used by Hodgkin and Huxley to discover the ionic basis of the action potential
Source: Courtesy of the National Institutes of Health History Office. Public Domain via Wikimedia Commons.

What they discovered in this living fiber defined modern neurophysiology. Hodgkin and Huxley observed that when a nerve is stimulated, the electrical potential across its membrane changes dramatically. At rest, the interior of the neuron is negatively charged relative to the outside environment −70 mV. But when activated, this voltage briefly reverses sign, rising to a positive value before returning to the resting state. This rapid wave of depolarization and repolarization propagates through the neuron like a pulse of energy. They called it an action potential. To the untrained eye, it's a fleeting blip on a graph, lasting only a millisecond. However, this brief pulse contains the fundamental unit of neural communication. Every thought, memory, and movement arises from countless such pulses, organized into structures of astonishing complexity.

The Ionic Mechanism: Physics Meets Biology

Hodgkin and Huxley's breakthrough was not only recording the action potential but also explaining it. They demonstrated that these impulses are generated by the movement of ionscharged particles such as sodium (Na^+) and potassium (K^+) across the neuron membrane. The cell membrane, once thought inert, turned out to be a living circuit board, studded with voltage-sensitive channels that open and close in response to tiny changes in voltage.

When a neuron is activated:

- Sodium channels open, allowing Na^+ ions to enter, increasing the cell's positive charge.

- Almost immediately, potassium channels open, allowing K^+ ions to exit, restoring the negative resting state.

This millisecond interval creates a self-propagating wave, a domino effect of electrical changes spreading along the axon. In 1952, Hodgkin and Huxley published their discoveries in a series of papers, describing this process in meticulous mathematical detail. Their ionic model not only explained neuronal activation but also provided a basis for mathematical modeling of neurons. For the first time, the electrical language of the brain could be expressed in equations.

Hodgkin and Huxley discovered that life is not static; it is a dynamic dance of voltages and ions. A neuron isn't simply alive; it repeatedly converts chemistry into information. This discovery has implications for digital immortality. Probably, if the essence of brain activity can be described physically and mathematically, then, at least in principle, it can be reproduced on another medium. Not perfectly, not trivially, but reproducibly. The action potential is both a biological fact and a symbol of possibility. It reminds us that consciousness, no matter how complex, arises from something measurable: waves of energy flowing through membranes over time. The mystery lies not in the brain producing electricity, but in how electricity produces thought. Hodgkin and Huxley were awarded the Nobel Prize in 1963, but their true legacy is both scientific and philosophical. They taught us that the mind is a system of patterns, and that these patterns, once understood, can one day be mapped, modeled, or even transferred.

Their work laid the foundation for computational neuroscience. By the 1960s, researchers were using the first computers to simulate neural activity, testing how networks of virtual neurons might behave.

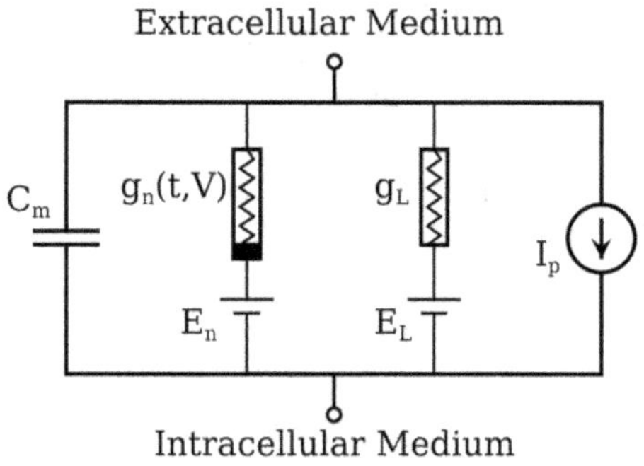

Figure 2.3 The Hodgkin–Huxley model represents the neuron membrane as an electrical circuit

The lipid bilayer behaves like a capacitor storing charge, ion channels act as conductances controlling current flow, electrochemical gradients function like batteries that drive ion movement, and ion pumps maintain these gradients. Together, these elements generate the electrical signals that propagate along neurons.

Source: Image by Krishnavedala, 2012, via Wikimedia Commons. Licensed under CC0 1.0 Universal Public Domain Dedication.

Brains as Information Processors

The next big leap, however, wasn't about what the brain looked like, or just what it did, but about what it meant. Scientists began asking a radical, almost audacious, question: could thinking itself be understood as a form of information processing? This idea, both elegant and revolutionary, suggested that underlying the chemistry and electricity of neurons lay a kind of code, a hidden pattern, a logic of signals and connections that could, in principle, be studied independently of their physical medium. It proposed that the mind might not simply be matter in motion, but a structure of interconnections and transformations, an abstract system of computation and communication. In this vision, the brain became not just a biological organ but a meaning machine, a network where electricity, chemistry, and connections converge to generate thought.

In the 1940s, the word "information" acquired a new, rigorous meaning. Physicist Claude Shannon, working at Bell Labs, developed a mathematical theory of communication as a way to measure the amount of information in a signal, the level of noise it could tolerate, and the efficiency of its transmission (Shannon, 1948). For Shannon, information had nothing to do with meaning or content, but with pattern. It could be quantified in bits, regardless of the medium. Whether it propagated as sound waves through the air, voltage through wires, or electrical impulses through neurons, the same abstract essence remained: information stripped down to its essence, as the measurable structure of signals. This represented a conceptual shift. If information existed independent of its medium, then perhaps the mind, the pattern of connections between neurons, could also exist independent of the physical brain.

At the same time, a group of pioneers, Norbert Wiener, Warren McCulloch, and Walter Pitts, were laying the foundations of cybernetics, a new science of control and communication in both machines and living organisms (Cope & Kalantzis, 2022). McCulloch and Pitts proposed a simple yet powerful mathematical model of a neuron: a switch that operates only when the incoming signal exceeds a certain threshold. McCulloch and Pitts proposed that networks of such neurons were, in principle, capable of performing any computations accessible to the human mind. This was a bold claim, linking biology and logic, matter and mathematics, into a single theoretical model. Wiener developed these ideas philosophically, emphasizing that biological and mechanical systems obey the same fundamental laws of feedback and information flow. For the first time, neurons and circuits, mind and computers, could be described in the same language. The boundaries between biology and computing began to change, hinting at a future in which the brain could be viewed not simply as tissue, but as a system for processing, transmitting, and transforming information (Adamson et al., 2015).

The Brain as Computer

When Santiago Ramón y Cajal peered through his microscope, he saw art, delicate, branching trees of neurons woven into vast networks of communication. Two generations later, Alan Turing, studying logic and mathematics, saw something entirely different: computation. Yet both were searching for the same secret: how does complexity arise from simplicity? How do small, discrete elements, be they neurons or symbols, combine to produce intelligence, thought, and understanding? At this intersection of biology and computation, a new idea was born: perhaps it was possible to model thought itself. Neural circuits and logical operations were not simply objects of study; they were templates, windows into the architecture of the mind. In their union, models of life and models of logic hinted at a deeper principle: the mechanics of thought could, in principle, be formalized, modeled, and even reproduced.

The Mathematical Brain

In 1943, Warren McCulloch and Walter Pitts published a paper that changed the course of science: "A Logical Calculus of the Ideas Immanent in Nervous Activity." In just 20 pages, they advanced a radical idea: the brain could be viewed as a logical network, a system of neurons performing computations (McCulloch & Pitts, 1943). Each neuron, they argued, receives signals from others, sums them, and activates when a threshold is reached. This activation, in turn, becomes an input signal for other neurons, creating a cascade of activity. The result is a network of logical operations, where every thought, perception, and action arises from the interaction of neurons turning on and off. Their model was primitive by today's standards, but its message was revolutionary: if neurons can compute, so can a machine.

While McCulloch and Pitts were describing biological computation, Alan Turing was imagining artificial computation. By 1936, he had already formulated the concept of a universal machine, a device capable of performing any computation given the right instructions. Later, he posed a deeper and more provocative question: "Can machines think?" Turing proposed this experiment not to define the concept of "thinking," but to test it: if a machine can convincingly imitate human conversation, who can say it isn't intelligent? His "Imitation Game," later known as the Turing Test, became the philosophical cornerstone of AI (Turing, 1950). While Ramón y Cajal and Hodgkin uncovered the physical structure of the brain, and McCulloch and Pitts modeled its logical architecture, Turing proposed a unifying idea: intelligence as computation.

The First Neural Networks

By the late 1950s, the dream of modeling thought began to take concrete shape. Psychologist Frank Rosenblatt created the perceptron, a simplified model of a neuron implemented in hardware. It could learn to recognize patterns, such as shapes or letters, through training. Rosenblatt's perceptron was limited, but it nonetheless represented the first true attempt at machine learning (Rosenblatt, 1962). Inspired by biology, it reflected the mechanism by which neural connections strengthen or weaken with experience. Rosenblatt envisioned a future in which perceptron networks could "walk, talk, see, write, reproduce themselves, and be aware of their own existence." For a time, the world believed him. Then came disillusionment. In 1969, Marvin Minsky and Seymour Papert published *Perceptrons*, showing that such networks were mathematically incapable of solving certain complex problems, even simple ones like the exclusive-OR (XOR) gate, and funding for neural networks dried up (Minsky & Papert, 1969). AI entered its first "AI winter." The dream of simulating the brain seemed naive, even arrogant. The metaphor of the mind as a machine seemed too far-fetched.

However, science is cyclical. Even as AI faded into the background, neuroscience advanced rapidly, uncovering the true mechanisms of brain learning: synaptic plasticity, feedback loops, and multilayer networks. These ideas, once fully understood, subsequently inspired the deep learning revolution, half a century after Rosenblatt first envisioned the perceptron.

From Biology to Machines

In the 1980s, Geoffrey Hinton, David Rumelhart, and James McClelland revived the neural idea with backpropagation, an algorithm that allowed networks to adjust their internal weights through error correction (Green, 2022). The principle was simple: machines could learn from mistakes, just as the brain strengthens useful connections and prunes unnecessary ones. This innovation revived the analogy between neurons and algorithms—not just as a metaphor, but as a computational principle based on learning. In the following decades, the development of connectionism transformed our understanding of intelligence. Instead of relying on central rules, cognition was viewed as the result of distributed interactions among many simple units—a model mirroring biology, where thought emerges from the collective behavior of billions of neurons.

By the 2010s, advances in computing power and massive data sets allowed deep learning to fulfill the promise of its pioneers. Neural networks could now see, speak, translate, play games, and even generate images and text. The line between organic and synthetic intelligence grew ever thinner as machines began to approach human cognition. Perhaps a poetic expression could be put this way: the more we teach machines to think, the more we realize how little we understand our own minds. Artificial neural networks learn differently from the brain, yet they exhibit parallel structures of abstraction and pattern recognition.

What We Know and What We Don't Know

Today, we can measure electrical activity in real time, map neural circuits with microscopic precision, and even predict behavior based on activation patterns. However, despite these remarkable achievements, something crucial still eludes us.

What we know:

- The brain is a physical system governed by the same laws of nature as all matter.
- The brain functions through electricity and chemistry, exchanging ions and neurotransmitters, activating in coordinated rhythms.
- Neurons form networks (which change) that store and process information.
- We can trace neural processes from sensory input to motor output.
- Perception begins with the activation of sensory neurons, which can be detected.
- Decisions are made by competing neural groups that integrate signals.
- The action occurs due to the coordinated activity of the motor areas.
- We can even simulate parts of this activity on computers—neural networks that simulate recognition, memory, and learning.
- When you see a face, your visual cortex is activated in a predictable way.
- When you remember something, a corresponding pattern of activation occurs.

What we don't know:

- This is the difficult problem of consciousness: how subjective experience arises from objective matter.
- We can measure neural activity, but we cannot measure self-awareness itself.
- We can detect patterns, but we cannot perceive them first-person.
- Even something as seemingly simple as visual perception remains a mystery.
- When you look at a tree, your brain processes light, color, and shape. But nowhere in these mechanisms can we find the "image" of the tree that you perceive in your mind's eye.
- No internal screen—no internal projector. And yet, somehow, you see.
- What is memory, and how is it stored?

While our current understanding is a blend of hard-won knowledge and persistent mysteries, we possess the intellectual and technological tools to move forward. Though we are often humbled by the "unknown," our progress is defined by a more vital achievement: we have finally begun to ask the right questions.

The Rise of Brain Imaging (fMRI, EEG, MEG)

We saw how mid-century pioneers such as Wiener, Shannon, Hodgkin, and Huxley reimagined the brain, imagining it as a site of intense information exchange. They gave us the logic of a "living circuit," after which we needed to find a way to observe its operation without breaking it. For centuries, the brain revealed its secrets only on the dissecting table. The real breakthrough in modern neurophysiology was not simply theorizing about these electrical impulses, but finally learning to listen to them in real time. This is where the history of neuroimaging begins. If we are to move from merely theorizing about the mind to actually capturing its data, we require tools capable of translating these silent biological pulses into a language we can finally record and analyze.

EEG: The Brain's Whisper Made Audible

The simplest and most widely used method, due to its simplicity, is the EEG. If you're looking to buy a device for reading brain signals, it will usually be an EEG device.

EEG (electroencephalography) records the brain's electrical rhythms. By placing electrodes on the scalp, we can measure voltage fluctuations during the synchronous activation of neurons. The resulting waves, alpha, beta, delta, theta, are like musical notes, informing us of the tempo and mood of the mind. EEG is a fast method capable of tracking events within milliseconds, but its spatial resolution is limited: we see the time of activity, but not its exact location.

The story began in 1913 when Vladimir Práwdicz-Neminski published the first electroencephalogram recorded from a dog's brain. He did this without damaging the animal's scalp, using a string galvanometer (Brigo, 2025). But real progress began in the 1920s with Hans Berger, the same man whose experiments marked the birth of neuroscience as a study of the brain. Working alone, driven by both scientific obsession and a personal interest in thinking, Berger attached electrodes to his head and recorded faint voltage fluctuations (Gloor, 1969). Berger discovered rhythmic patterns in waves that rose and fell when the subject was resting, concentrating, or falling asleep. He called them alpha waves, and they became the first glimpses of the electrical rhythm of the living mind. Thousands of researchers still use alpha rhythms in their research. Data processing is improving, but so is the essence of the process.

The device he uses, an EEG, is deceptively simple: a set of electrodes, amplifiers, and recording paper (or, as is common today, a digital interface). But what it captures is truly amazing—the synchronized activation of millions of neurons, a chorus of waves on the brain's surface, harmonized into waves of measurable frequency.

It could determine when something was happening in the brain, but not where.

Nevertheless, EEG was pioneered and found widespread medical applications in the study of diseases such as epilepsy and autism. The invisible now became recordable, measurable, and living.

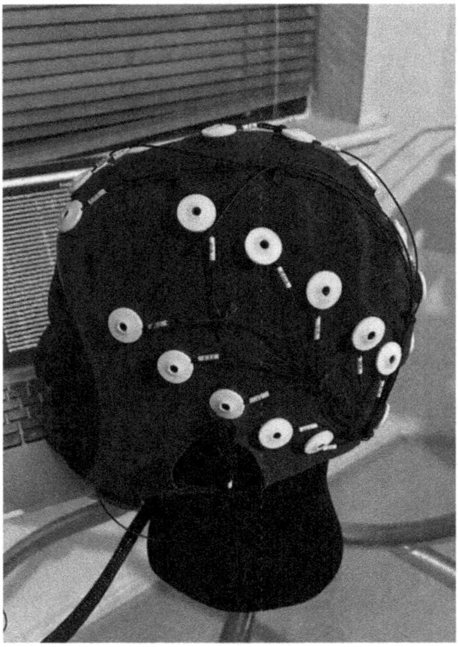

Figure 2.4 An EEG cap with electrodes is used to record the brain's electrical rhythms

Touch a Brain: Invasive Way

However, despite its value, noninvasive EEG is subject to filtering—its signals are blurred and softened as they pass through bone and tissue, producing a broad but fuzzy image.

Invasive path overcomes this barrier. By placing electrodes directly on the cortex or deep within the brain, it captures the electrical impulse of thought at its source. Each contact records, with astonishing clarity, the coordinated activation of neurons, the rise and fall of oscillations underlying sensations, decisions, and movements. What noninvasive EEG perceives as a distant flicker, invasive methods transform into complex structure and synchronization. This precision has made invasive electrodes indispensable for identifying epileptic foci, planning neurosurgery, and deepening our understanding of how neural circuits shape behavior and consciousness (Hochberg et al., 2006).

In recent years, pioneers like Elon Musk have expanded the applications of invasive technology beyond medicine. Thanks to Neuralink (https://neuralink.com/) and similar projects, the goal is now not just recording but transmitting information—creating brain–computer interfaces capable of restoring lost functions and, ultimately, linking the human mind to digital systems.

Invasive method represents both the culmination and evolution of centuries of electrophysiological research. It bridges the gap between observation and participation, transforming electrical activity into a dialogue. And yet, even as

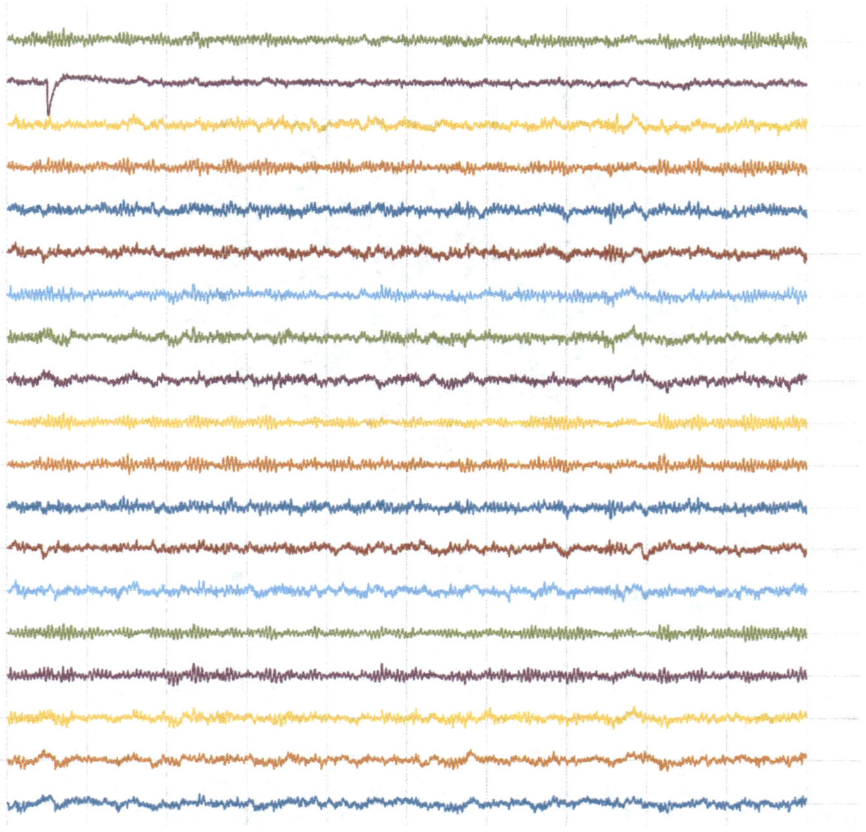

Figure 2.5 Example of EEG data
Source: Reproduced from "Diagnosis of Schizophrenia Using EEG Sensor Data," by S. Aziz, et al., 2024, *Sensors, 24*(20), 650, doi:10.3390/s24206508, CC BY 4.0.

we learn to listen more closely to the brain's inner voice, a deeper question remains: will understanding the code of thought ever fully reveal the experience encoded within? Indeed, when we see news of someone sending messages with a robotic hand using the power of thought, it was typically achieved through invasive technologies.

While invasive electrodes provide access to the brain's electrical landscape, their capabilities are limited by both biology and technology. The implantation process itself disrupts the delicate balance of neural tissue: electrodes penetrate networks densely populated not only by neurons but also by glial cells, astrocytes, microglia, and oligodendrocytes that support and protect the neural environment. Their activation in response to foreign materials can lead to inflammation, gliosis, and gradual signal degradation over time. What initially provides a window into the brain's internal processes can gradually become obscured by the body's defense mechanisms (Barrese et al., 2013).

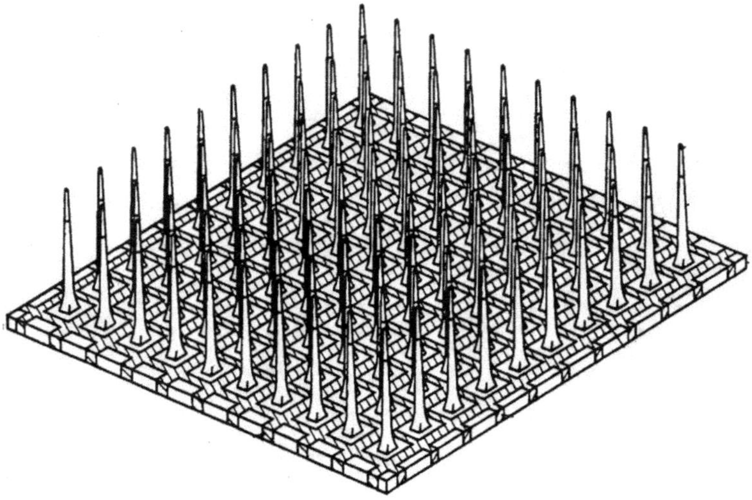

Figure 2.6 Schematic electrode array for direct connection with brain
Source: Adapted from U.S. Patent No. 5,215,088, "Three-dimensional electrode device," by R. A. Normann, 1993. Wikipedia, Public Domain.

Furthermore, the spatial coverage of invasive electrodes is inherently limited. Each electrode records signals from a tiny cluster of neurons, providing precise local detail but a fragmented picture of the global network. The brain's extensive connections and its dynamic interactions between the cortex and subcortical regions often elude such limited recordings. Even advanced multi-electrode arrays face a tradeoff between resolution, stability, and biocompatibility. Ethical and practical concerns also remain: surgical risks, long-term consequences of implantation, and the interpretation of vast neural data sets that we only partially understand. Despite these limitations, the invasive way remains a vital tool for dialogue between biology and engineering. It reminds us that the brain is not simply an electrical circuit, but living tissue whose complexity defies full measurement even by the most advanced instruments.

MEG: Listening to the Magnetic Echo

Many of us have probably seen large machines, at least in films, where people are placed inside. As technology advanced, scientists began to ask a new question: if neurons generate electric fields, could they also create magnetic ones? This was a natural extension of Ramón y Cajal's vision and an evolution from the microscopic to the invisible. If the brain is a number of electrical impulses, perhaps its collective work also generated a subtle magnetic effect in the space around the skull.

In the 1960s and 1970s, this idea took physical form in a revolutionary device: magnetoencephalography (MEG). It was based on a sophisticated invention, a SQUID (squirt magnetometer), or superconducting quantum interference device capable of detecting magnetic flux variations as small as one billionth of the Earth's own magnetic field. In 1968, David Cohen recorded the first magnetoencephalogram (MEG) using a copper induction coil in a magnetically shielded room (Cohen, 1968). The subsequent integration of the Superconducting Quantum Interference Device (SQUID), developed by James Zimmerman, revolutionized the field (Zimmerman et al., 1970). For the first time, scientists were able to detect magnetic echoes of thought itself. Where EEG measures brain voltage, MEG records its magnetic resonance. Together, they offered two complementary views of the same event—one electrical, the other magnetic; two signatures of a neural storm. However, MEG added a dimension that EEG could not. Its sensitivity provided not only millisecond temporal precision but also an unprecedented ability to localize activity deep within the brain. Now researchers could map in real time how signals originate, propagate, and interact between brain regions. MEG revealed the hidden choreography of the brain—the split-second interactions between sensory areas, the cascade of activity that transforms perception into awareness. What were once static snapshots of brain function became moving images, dynamic stories unfolding in real time. For neuroscientists, it was like replacing a stethoscope with a camera—an instrument that not only heard the rhythms of the mind but also observed their dance.

MEG marked another turning point in a long journey that began with electricity, magnets, and the study of neurons. It bridged physics and biology, transforming invisible fields into data, and data into understanding. Every advance from Galvani's frogs to Ramón y Cajal's neurons and modern neuroimaging brought us closer to understanding the mind as matter, and image as signal and structure.

And yet, with each level of measurement, the mystery deepens. The more precisely we can track the brain's flickering fields, the more elusive consciousness itself seems—still flickering beyond the reach of our instruments.

fMRI: Observing the Brain's Thinking

Functional magnetic resonance imaging (fMRI) does not directly capture the physical firing of individual neurons. Instead, it maps brain activity by monitoring the hemodynamic response—the subtle shift in blood flow that accompanies neuronal activation. Because active neurons demand increased oxygen, the system tracks fluctuations in blood oxygen levels to identify which cortical regions are engaged during specific tasks.

This breakthrough was made possible by Seiji Ogawa, who recognized that MRI could reveal more than just static anatomical structures. Ogawa discovered that deoxyhemoglobin acts as a paramagnetic agent, essentially serving as a tiny magnet that disrupts the MRI signal (Ogawa et al., 1990). When neurons fire, the vascular system overcompensates by delivering a surge of oxygenated blood; this "flushes" the magnetic interference and causes the active areas to appear brighter on the scan.

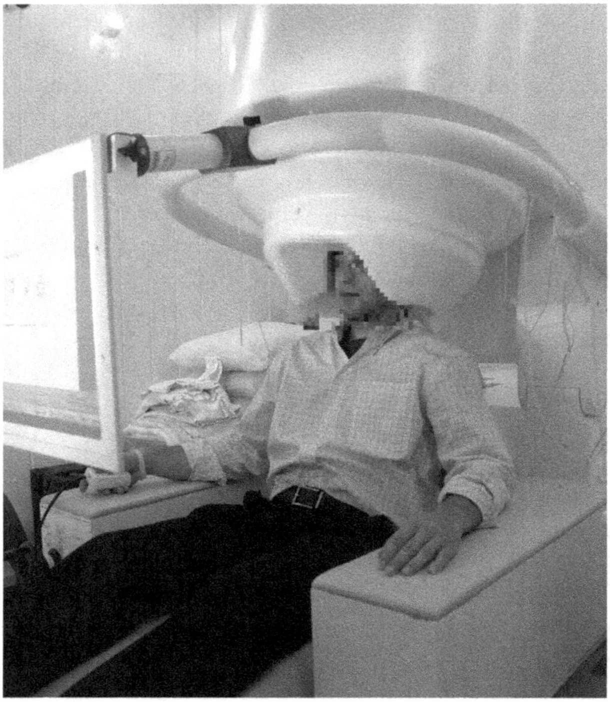

Figure 2.7 A subject undergoing an MEG scan
Source: National Institute of Mental Health (NIMH). Public Domain via Wikimedia Commons.

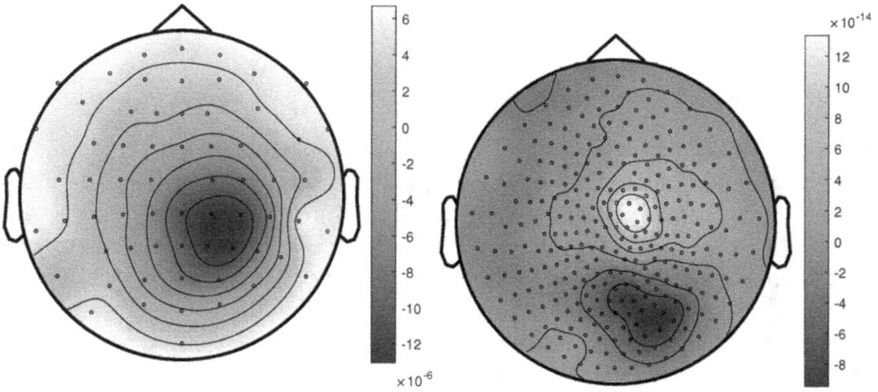

Figure 2.8 Example of MEG data
Source: Neugebauer et al., *Brain Sciences* 2022, 12, 114; Used under CC BY 4.0.

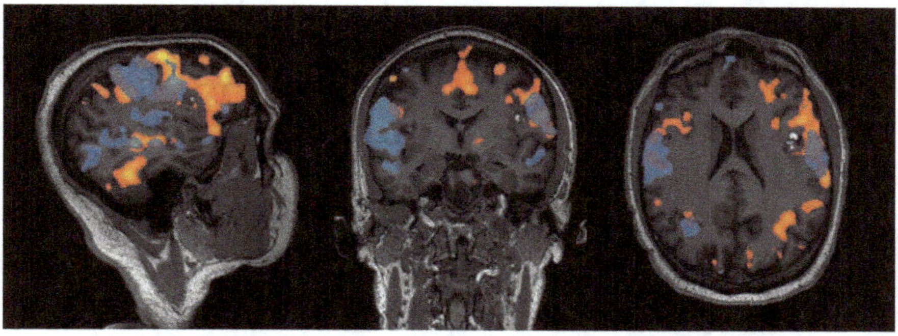

Figure 2.9 Example of *fMRI* image
Source: Sighinolfi et al., *Tomography* 2022, 8, 267–280. Used under CC BY 4.0.

By processing these metabolic signatures, powerful computers can reconstruct a living map of the mind in motion. Through this lens, the mind is transformed into a real-time narrative: as a subject speaks, remembers, or dreams, specific cortical regions flicker across the display like tiny galaxies of activation, appearing and fading in perfect synchronization with their thoughts.

The visual cortex brightened when subjects observed moving patterns. The amygdala lit up when they experienced fear. The prefrontal cortex pulsed as they made decisions or weighed moral choices. For centuries, philosophers could only guess at where thoughts originated. Now, researchers could point to images as proof that love, memory, or imagination had their place. Yet even in this triumph, a silent warning sounded. The vivid images of fMRI are not thoughts themselves, but echoes of statistical translations of changing oxygen levels, represented as gradients of light. A scan is not a mind; it is a map of energy consumption. To mistake it for the thing itself is to confuse shadow with substance, signal with meaning. Yet this tool transformed the landscape of neuroscience. Where once we dissected static organs, we could now observe the living interactions of their regions in real time.

Conclusion

While each imaging method has its own unique strengths and weaknesses, we must remember that they were originally developed for clinical medicine, not to decipher the essence of consciousness itself. We cannot simply accept these tools as the mind they measure; instead, modern researchers are creatively synthesizing these disparate technologies, bridging the gaps between them to finally shed light on the enduring mystery of our inner lives.

Even working with these tools, scientists conclude that the more precisely we measure brain function, the deeper the question becomes: how do these measurable processes generate experience, identity, and meaning? Each discovery narrows the gap between biology and computation, but also deepens our understanding of what remains unexplained.

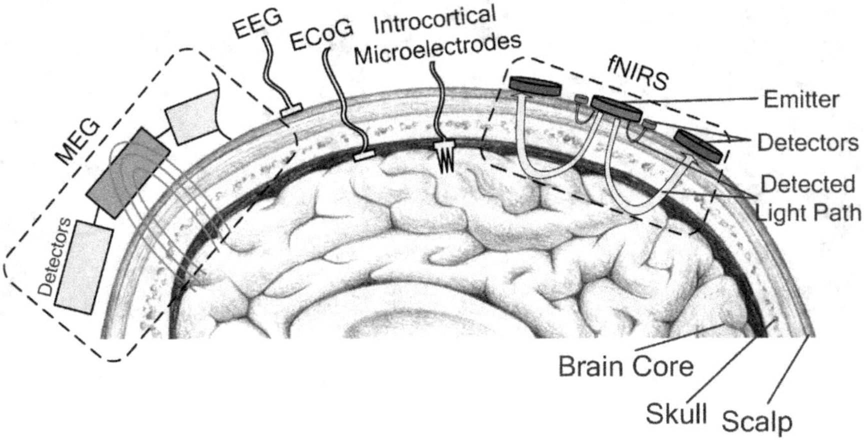

Figure 2.10 BCI sensor mounting types: invasive (IM), semi-invasive (ECoG), and non-invasive (MEG, EEG, fNIRS)

Source: Peksa, J., & Mamchur, D., *Sensors* 2023, 23(13), 6001; doi.org/10.3390/s23136001, CC BY 4.0.

References

Adamson, G., Kline, R. R., Michael, K., & Michael, M. G. (2015). Wiener's cybernetics legacy and the growing need for an interdisciplinary approach. *Proceedings of the IEEE*, 103(11), 2208–2214. doi:10.1109/JPROC.2015.2483958

Barrese, J. C., Rao, N., Paroo, K., Triebwasser, C., Vargas-Irwin, C., Franquemont, L., & Donoghue, J. P. (2013). Failure mode analysis of silicon-based intracortical microelectrode arrays in non-human primates. *Journal of Neural Engineering*, 10(6), Article 066014. doi:10.1088/1741-2560/10/6/066014

Brigo, F. (2025). Precursors of clinical electroencephalography: from animal electricity to brain wave recording. In: Brigo, F., & Mecarelli, O. (eds) *EEG: The first 100 years*. Springer. doi:10.1007/978-3-031-86878-8_1

Cohen, D. (1968). Magnetoencephalography: Evidence of magnetic fields produced by alpha-rhythm currents. *Science*, 161(3843), 784–786.

Cope, B., & Kalantzis, M. (2022). The cybernetics of learning. *Educational Philosophy and Theory*, 54(14), 2352–2388. doi:10.1080/00131857.2022.2033213

Gloor, P. (1969). Hans Berger on electroencephalography. *American Journal of EEG Technology*, 9(1), 1–8. doi:10.1080/00029238.1969.11080728

Green, C. D. (2022). *What kind of explanation, if any, is a connectionist net?* Cornell University Press.

Hochberg, L., Serruya, M., Friehs, G. et al. (2006). Neuronal ensemble control of prosthetic devices by a human with tetraplegia. *Nature*, 442, 164–171. doi:10.1038/nature04970

Hodgkin, A. L., & Huxley, A. F. (1952). A quantitative description of membrane current and its application to conduction and excitation in nerve. *The Journal of Physiology*, 117(4), 500–544.

McCulloch, W. S., & Pitts, W. (1943). A logical calculus of the ideas immanent in nervous activity. *The Bulletin of Mathematical Biophysics*, 5(4), 115–133.

Minsky, M. L., & Papert, S. A. (1969). *Perceptrons: An introduction to computational geometry*. MIT Press.

Ogawa, S., Lee, T. M., Kay, A. R., & Tank, D. W. (1990). Brain magnetic resonance imaging with contrast dependent on blood oxygenation. *Proceedings of the National Academy of Sciences*, 87(24), 9868–9872.

Ramón y Cajal, S. (1937). *Recollections of my life* (Trans. E. Horne Craigie). American Philosophical Society. [This is the "gold standard" source for his personal history.]

Rosenblatt, F. (1962). *Principles of neurodynamics: Perceptrons and the theory of brain mechanisms*. Spartan Books.

Shannon, C. E. (1948). A mathematical theory of communication. *The Bell System Technical Journal*, 27(3), 379–423. doi:10.1002/j.1538-7305.1948.tb01338.x

Turing, A. M. (1950). Computing machinery and intelligence. *Mind*, 59(236), 433–460. doi:10.1093/mind/LIX.236.433

Zimmerman, J. E., Thiene, P., & Harding, J. T. (1970). Design and operation of stable rf-biased superconducting point-contact quantum devices, and a note on the properties of perfectly-clean metal contacts. *Journal of Applied Physics*, 41(4), 1572–1580.

3 Consciousness

The Hard Problem

Introduction

Here we'll step away from the technical aspects and consider a more abstract question: what does digital immortality actually mean? To understand this, we first need to understand what exactly needs to be copied or transmitted, and what we know about it.

Digital immortality depends on artificial intelligence (AI), but before we can imagine its creation, we need to understand what exactly is being created. If we expect such a system to preserve humans, it must possess some kind of consciousness. But what is consciousness? The question seems simple at first glance, but once you begin to look for a deeper reason, you find yourself in increasingly complex territory, full of new questions. Consciousness is familiar, ever-present, seemingly obvious until we try to explain it in detail.

We experience consciousness in every waking moment: the sensation of being, the perception of the world, the texture of sensations, the flow of thought. But the main paradox is that, despite centuries of research, science still cannot fully explain how physical matter generates subjective experience, how patterns become experience. How does the activation of billions of neurons transform into the redness of red, the feeling of friendship, and the trace of memories?

Modern neuroscience operates within the framework of physicalism, the idea that everything, including the mind, arises from physical processes. If the brain is an electrochemical machine, then consciousness should, in principle, be explainable in these terms. However, even within this framework, we face an explanatory gap. Knowing the position and firing rate of each neuron does not automatically reveal the system's experience. A brain map is not the mind itself.

This gap poses one of the most serious challenges to the dream of mind uploading. If we don't understand consciousness, how can we hope to replicate it? Even if a digital brain perfectly replicates the structure and activity of the human brain, will it truly be conscious or simply behave as if it were? This question is not only scientific but also existential. It touches on questions of identity, morality, and the boundaries of life itself.

DOI: 10.4324/9781003794677-4

Some scientists argue that consciousness may not be a single phenomenon at all, but a collection of processes, perception, memory, attention, and self-modeling that together create the illusion of a unified self (Graziano, 2022).

Others suggest that consciousness may be a fundamental property of the universe, like space or time, irreducible to physical mechanisms. Between these extremes lies a vast field of research that combines neuroscience, physics, philosophy, and even information theory. We will examine modern theories in the sections that follow. In any case, to create a digital mind, we must first understand what a mind is.

The Tale of Two Problems: Function vs. Feeling

For much of the 20th century, scientists believed that if we could just map the brain's "wiring," the mystery of the mind would vanish. This gave rise to what we now call the **"Soft Problems"** of consciousness. These are the questions of function: how does the brain integrate information, how do we focus our attention, and how do we translate sensory input into motor output? These problems are "soft" not because they are easy, but because they have a clear path to a solution through biology and engineering.

However, in the 1990s, philosopher David Chalmers pointed out a glaring "explanatory gap" in this success story. He argued that even if we solved every soft problem, even if we knew the position and firing rate of every single neuron, we would still be left with the **"Hard Problem"** (Chalmers, 1996). The Hard Problem: this is the "why" of the brain. It asks why all that data processing is accompanied by a subjective "inner light." It is the difference between a computer that "identifies" the color red and a human who "experiences" the redness of red

From Theory to Tissue: The Biological Blueprint

While the "hard problem" haunts philosophers, neuroscientists often take a more pragmatic approach. To solve the mystery of the mind, they look toward the physical structures that might house it. When tackling such a large-scale problem, it's often best to start with the simplest forms of life, for example, by studying the neurons of a whale or the primitive nervous system of a mollusk. We operate under the assumption that consciousness originates in the brain, and that this biological machinery is what defines us as "alive."

However, nature reveals a startling truth: not all living things possess consciousness as we understand it. Consider the common garden slug (Godfrey-Smith, 2021). These simple mollusks lack a centralized brain; instead, they operate through a decentralized network of nerve nodes known as ganglia. These clusters allow them to navigate their environment, locate food, and retreat from predators with surprising efficiency.

To an observer, the slug's behavior seems almost robotic, yet we instinctively perceive it as a living entity. This distinction is crucial for our digital quest: slugs remind us that life and intelligence are not synonymous. A slug's body can

Figure 3.1 The Roman snail (Helix pomatia), a member of the class Gastropoda
Source: Photo by Jürgen Schöner, 2009, CC BY-SA 3.0, Wikipedia.

perform complex actions, including navigation and rudimentary memory, without a central "ego" to oversee them. In a sense, these creatures are living algorithms, proof that nature can achieve survival and adaptation without the need for a subjective "inner light."

Many Brains: The Distributed Mind

If the slug represents a life form that thrives without a central command center, the cephalopod represents an even more radical departure from the human template. While we are used to thinking of the "self" as a single pilot sitting in the cockpit of the skull, nature has drafted a very different blueprint for high-level intelligence.

If slugs survive without a central brain, others take the opposite approach: distributing their intelligence across multiple neural nodes. The octopus is the crowning example of this biological "mesh network." Its central brain is located in its head, but nearly two-thirds of its neurons are actually located in its arms. Each of its eight limbs contains its own "mini-brain" capable of independent movement, learning, and even decision-making. Similarly, certain worms, starfish, and other mollusks possess decentralized nervous systems that coordinate complex behaviors without a single, stifling point of control.

These animals challenge our fundamental ideas about how intelligence and consciousness must be structured. Each arm of an octopus can solve problems like unscrewing a jar or mimicking a predator without the direct involvement of the central brain. This distributed thinking enables remarkable flexibility: they can camouflage their skin, escape from high-security enclosures, and explore their environment in multiple directions simultaneously. Essentially, their bodies house multiple semi-independent minds (this is functional decentralization, not literal plural selves) that seamlessly interact in a form of biological multitasking that far exceeds human capability (Godfrey-Smith, 2018).

From a philosophical and scientific perspective, these creatures raise profound questions: Is consciousness necessarily unified? Can multiple "subminds" constitute a single self, or do they represent a networked form of life fundamentally different from our own?

Figure 3.2 The common octopus (Octopus vulgaris)
Source: Illustration by Giacomo Merculiano from *The Fauna and Flora of the Gulf of Naples*, 1896. Public Domain, available via Wikimedia Commons.

When it comes to the dream of digital immortality, the octopus provides a vital clue. It hints at the possibility of a mind that is not only stored but distributed, perhaps existing simultaneously across multiple nodes, machines, or even separate robotic bodies. In the study of life and the quest for the eternal, these "many-brained" wonders prove there is no single template for intelligence. Evolution has already mastered the art of the network. If intelligence can be distributed in nature, it might also be distributed in silicon.

For our purposes, these examples serve as a reminder: achieving immortality, whether biological or digital, may require us to think beyond the confines of the human "ego" trapped in a single skull. Perhaps the digital future of the mind is not a single thread of consciousness, but a vast, thriving network that defies our current intuition.

Why Consciousness Matters

Even if we could map every neuron in your brain and reproduce its connections within a machine, what would that copy actually be? Would it wake up? Would it be aware of itself as you are with your memories, emotions, and sense of continuity, or would it simply act as if it knew you?

At first glance, the difference may seem abstract. But imagine standing before your digital double: it speaks like you, remembers your childhood, and insists on experiencing happiness, curiosity, and fear. To an observer, the distinction between the original and the copy may seem meaningless. However, from your perspective, there is a significant difference: you are still standing there, observing. What operates within the machine may not be an extension of your consciousness, but the birth of an entirely new one.

This is why consciousness cannot be reduced to simple information. Information describes structure and function, but not experience. Similarly, a perfectly reconstructed mind may still lack a crucial component of subjective experience that makes consciousness real. Without it, digital immortality becomes an illusion: eternal life without awareness.

Science has made big strides in transcript thought patterns. We can now detect when someone is asleep, recognize specific memories from neural signatures, and even reconstruct rough images from brain activity. But these achievements, impressive as they may be, remain only external views of the mind. They tell us about what the brain does, not what it is like to be that brain. The internal dimension "what it's like" remains hidden from objective measurement.

This raises a disturbing possibility: perhaps consciousness cannot be uploaded because it is not a thing in the usual sense. It may exist not as data, but as a dynamic process that arises only in certain physical systems that live, communicate, and feel. If this is true, then transferring your mind into a machine will not preserve you; it will merely create a simulation, a shadow that mimics your thoughts but never shares your consciousness.

Yet others argue the opposite. If the mind truly is information patterns of connections, signal sequences, feedback loops, and representations, then copying it should, in principle, reproduce the same conscious experience. From this perspective, consciousness is not tied to biology, but to the computation itself. A silicon neuron, if it behaved identically to a biological one, could possess the same consciousness. The substrate is irrelevant; only the pattern matters.

Between these two perspectives lies the key moment of the debate: is consciousness an emergent property of complex computation, or is it something more, something that cannot be captured by replication alone? The answer may determine whether digital immortality is achievable or forever out of reach.

When we talk about mind uploading, we're not simply asking how to copy information. We're asking what it means to *be*. Our goal isn't to increase memory capacity or speed up processors, but to understand the very essence of experience. If a digital copy can't experience joy, love, or wonder, then it's not an extension of humanity, it's a mirror reflecting us, even though it was never alive.

For this reason, consciousness is more important than any other factor in the dream of digital immortality. It is the dividing line between simulation and selfhood, between computation and life. Understanding it means unlocking not only the key to mind uploading, but also the deepest question: what makes us truly human?

Philosophical Foundations

Long before the advent of neuroscience and AI, consciousness was already one of humanity's most ancient mysteries. Philosophers, mystics, and scientists have all tried to answer the same question: what is the relationship between mind and matter? Is mind simply what the brain does, or is it something more, something irreducible, something that science alone cannot explain?

The modern debate began in the 17th century with the French philosopher René Descartes, who proclaimed, "Cogito, ergo sum"—"I think, therefore I am." From this starting point, Descartes proposed dualism, the idea that reality consisted of two fundamentally different substances: mind and matter (Descartes, 1641/1996). Matter was physical, extended, and subject to mechanical laws. Mind, by contrast, was immaterial, conscious, and indivisible. These two principles interacted somehow, most likely, Descartes believed, through the pineal gland (an endocrine gland that forms part of the epithalamus), but remained distinct.

Dualism was intuitively appealing. After all, our subjective experience feels entirely different from physical processes. The activation of neurons seems completely different from the sensation of pain, and the movement of atoms seems completely removed from the flow of thought. For centuries, this dualistic

Figure 3.3 René Descartes (1596–1650), a French philosopher who proposed dualism—the idea that the mind and body are fundamentally different substances
Source: Portrait by Frans Hals, c. 1649. Public domain via Wikimedia Commons.

view shaped both religion and philosophy, preserving the idea of the soul as something separate from the body, something that can even survive death.

However, as science developed, dualism began to lose its footing. The rise of materialism, the belief that everything in the universe, including consciousness, arises from physical processes, changed our understanding of the mind. According to materialism, the mind is not a separate substance, but an emergent property of brain activity. When neurons fire in a certain way, consciousness arises, just as moisture arises from the interaction of water molecules. There are no additional ingredients, no invisible soul, only complex matter generating experience.

Materialism fits well with the scientific worldview, but it has its own set of problems (Dennett, 1991). Chief among them is what philosophers call the explanatory gap—the difficulty of explaining why physical processes give rise to subjective experience at all.

It is here that contemporary philosophical debates are resurfacing with renewed vigor. In the 1990s, David Chalmers reformulated the question, distinguishing between the **"soft problems"** of consciousness, explaining perception, cognition, and attention, and the **"hard problem"**: explaining why these processes are accompanied by subjective experience (Chalmers, 1996). Why should any information-processing system have an inner life? Why does consciousness exist at all, if the universe could, in principle, exist without it? Chalmers's formulation has revived the debate, dividing scientists and philosophers into two broad camps. On one side are materialists and reductionists, who believe that consciousness will eventually be fully explained in physical or computational terms, and that the "hard problem" is difficult only because we don't yet have the right theories. On the other side are dual aspect theorists, panpsychists, and property dualists, who suggest that consciousness may be a fundamental feature of reality, not derivable from anything else.

Some, such as Thomas Nagel, have argued that science can never fully grasp consciousness because it is inherently subjective, it has a "point of view." His famous essay "What Is It Like to Be a Bat?" points out that no objective data can tell us what it's like to be another being. In this sense, consciousness can resist objectification because it is defined by its first-person quality (Nagel, 1974). Others take a bolder position. Panpsychism, for example, proposes that consciousness is not an emergent but a universal property that every particle of matter possesses some tiny spark of experience, and that human consciousness is simply a highly organized expression of this universal capacity for sentience (Goff, 2019). While this idea sounds radical, it has rekindled the interest of philosophers and even some neuroscientists seeking to bridge this explanatory gap.

For the dream of mind uploading, these philosophical contradictions aren't academic, but fundamental. If materialism is true and consciousness arises solely from physical interactions, then theoretically, a sufficiently detailed digital copy of the brain could also be conscious. But if dualism or panpsychism contains even a grain of truth, then consciousness could depend on something that cannot be copied, a quality inherent in the living substrate or even the very fabric of the universe.

Therefore, any attempt to recreate or transfer the mind must face not only technical but also metaphysical limitations. The question is not only whether we can upload the brain, but also whether consciousness will follow or be left behind.

Neuroscientific Theories of Consciousness

Philosophy asks why consciousness exists; neuroscience asks how it exists. In recent decades, scientists have been attempting to translate centuries-old abstract reasoning into empirical models that could, in principle, explain how subjective experience arises from neural activity. While no single theory has yet achieved universal acceptance, three have become particularly influential: Global Workspace Theory, Integrated Information Theory, and Predictive Processing theory. Each offers a unique perspective on the mystery of consciousness, and each has profound implications for our dream of reconstructing the mind.

Global Workspace Theory (Baars, Dehaene)

If the brain is a vast theater, countless unconscious processes, such as perception, memory, emotion, and language, occur behind the scenes, vying for the spotlight. Most of them remain offstage, invisible to conscious awareness. But when one process "wins," it moves to the illuminated center of the stage, becoming conscious. This is the essence of Global Workspace Theory (GWT), first proposed by cognitive scientist Bernard Baars (Baars, 1988) in the 1980s and later expanded upon by neuroscientist Stanislas Dehaene (Dehaene, 2014).

According to GWT, consciousness isn't present everywhere in the brain; it arises when information is globally transmitted across multiple networks. When you become aware of a sound or thought, this information is distributed across systems responsible for decision-making, memory, and language, allowing it to guide behavior. From this perspective, the brain's unconscious modules are like specialized actors, and consciousness is the stage on which they share their results.

Dehaene and his colleagues found support for this model using neuroimaging and EEG. When a stimulus is consciously perceived—for example, a word flashing long enough to be noticed—it triggers a sudden, widespread burst of activity in the cerebral cortex, a pattern known as the "P3 wave." This synchronized activation corresponds to the entry of information into the global workspace, making it accessible to the entire cognitive system.

In the context of mind uploading, GWT offers a compelling mechanistic view of consciousness: a dynamic broadcast network that could, in principle, be simulated. If a digital brain could replicate the same architecture with individual modules and a central workspace, perhaps consciousness could emerge there too. However, GWT also hints at a limitation: consciousness depends not on input, but on integration and accessibility. Simply copying the brain's structure may not recreate the coordinated dance required for awareness.

Integrated Information Theory (Tononi)

While GWT focuses on the flow of information, Integrated Information Theory (IIT), proposed by neuroscientist Giulio Tononi, focuses on its structure (Tononi, 2004). IIT is based on a simple yet radical postulate: consciousness corresponds to a system's ability to integrate information. The more integrated and irreducible a system's informational connections are, the richer its experience.

In AI, consciousness is not associated with computations or functions, but with causal interdependence. A system is conscious to the extent that its parts cannot be separated without losing information about the whole. Tononi quantifies this using a mathematical measure called Φ *(phi)*, the amount of integrated information in a network. A system with a high Φ (e.g., the human brain) has a high degree of unification, while a system with a low Φ (e.g., a simple computer circuit) has little or no consciousness.

This approach is attractive because it attempts to go beyond metaphor and directly measure consciousness. It even makes testable predictions: for example, during deep sleep or anesthesia, Φ decreases, corresponding to a decrease in awareness. In principle, a digital system with a sufficiently high Φ could also possess consciousness.

However, IIT also raises serious philosophical and practical questions. If every system with integrated information possesses some degree of consciousness, then even simple circuits may possess a weak inner life, a view reminiscent of panpsychism. Moreover, calculating Φ for complex networks like the human brain is computationally difficult; no one yet knows how to measure it in real time.

For the mind uploading project, IIT presents a double-edged sword. On the one hand, it offers a potential metric for consciousness, suggesting that we will one day be able to verify whether a digital brain is truly conscious. On the other hand, it implies that consciousness may depend on the specific causal structure of the biological brain, not just its functions. A simulation can reproduce the output, but not the integrated causal relationships that make experience possible.

Models of Predictive Information Processing

A new and increasingly influential view regards the brain not as a passive receiver of information, but as an active predictive machine. According to the predictive information processing (PIP) hypothesis, or the Bayesian brain hypothesis, consciousness arises from the brain's constant efforts to minimize surprise to predict sensory information and update its internal model of the world when these predictions fail.

From this standpoint, perception isn't the brain registering reality, but guessing it. You don't see the world directly; you see the brain's best guess about what's happening around you. The world appears stable and consistent because your brain constantly adjusts itself, integrating new sensory data into its predictive system.

How does this relate to consciousness? Some theorists, such as Karl Friston and Anil Seth, suggest that conscious experience corresponds to a fine balance between prediction and error (Friston, 2010). Consciousness, they argue, is the brain's real-time interaction between expectation and reality, a sense of the unfolding world as the brain updates its model of itself and its environment.

This model has profound implications for artificial consciousness. If consciousness emerges from predictive modeling, then creating a digital mind may require more than just mapping neurons, it will require endowing the system with self-generating expectations, a sense of its own body and environment, and the ability to update its beliefs about reality. In other words, to feel, a system must not only process information but also distinguish between prediction and truth.

The Challenge of Subjectivity

From an external, scientific perspective, consciousness can be described as electrical patterns in neural circuits or information integrated into networks. But no matter how detailed the map, the subjective "what it's like" remains invisible. No scan can reveal the feeling of pain; no algorithm can tell us what it's like to taste coffee.

The difficulty lies not in measuring activity, but in explaining why this activity is experienced as something internal. They could predict the dilation of your pupils, the firing rate of your visual cortex, the emotional response of your limbic system, but nowhere in this data would the beauty of the sunset be reflected. The experience is real, but it exists in a reality to which no external observer has access.

The paradox is that consciousness is simultaneously the most familiar and the most difficult phenomenon to explain, challenging the very methods of science. Science relies on objectivity, on a view from nowhere. Consciousness, by definition, is subjectivity, a view from somewhere within you. Connecting these two perspectives may require a new concept that can connect first- and third-person narratives without reducing one to the other.

Some researchers are attempting to bridge this gap. Neurophenomenology, inspired by the Chilean biologist, philosopher, cyberneticist, and neuroscientist Francisco Varela, combines subjective reports with neural data, asking participants to describe their experiences while their brains are monitored, identifying patterns linking the perceptual and the measurable (Varela et al, 2016). Others, such as Anil Seth, a British professor of cognitive and computational neuroscience, argue that consciousness is a controlled hallucination, the brain's best guess about reality, suggesting that subjectivity is not an obstacle, but a fundamental function of the brain (Seth, 2021). However, these are only the first steps toward a deeper synthesis that remains to be realized.

For the dream of mind uploading, the problem of subjectivity cuts to the core. Suppose we successfully copy every neuron, every synapse, and every connection in your brain into a computer. Even if this digital mind behaves exactly like you, even if it claims to feel, we'll still be faced with the intractable question: "Does it actually experience anything?" Or has it become an empty simulation, a perfect imitation without an inner life?

This is the eternal question of philosophical zombies, creatures indistinguishable from conscious humans but lacking subjective awareness. If such an entity is logically possible, then the project of reproducing consciousness becomes far more complex than simply reproducing neural function.

Subjectivity resists understanding because it is not an object among objects, it is the space in which all objects manifest. It is the lens through which reality is seen, and no description of this lens can replace the act of seeing. Until we find a way to connect the world of first-person experience with the world of third-person measurement, consciousness will remain, as Chalmers says, "a hard problem that refuses to be solved."

Functionalist Hope

According to functionalism, the dominant view in cognitive science, what matters is what a system does, not what it's made of. If consciousness arises from patterns of information processing, then any system implementing these patterns must be conscious regardless of whether it consists of neurons, transistors, or photonic qubits. According to this view, uploading consciousness is conceptually possible. Copy the patterns, preserve the personality (Sanches de Oliveira, 2022).

This optimism largely drives the interest in brain emulation and artificial general intelligence. The brain is viewed as a kind of biological computer, and if we can replicate its functional architecture, consciousness should emerge naturally. In this sense, uploading becomes not a philosophical impossibility, but an engineering challenge, a matter of resolution and precision.

However, not everyone agrees that consciousness is a purely computational problem. Many scientists and philosophers argue that consciousness is embodied and inseparable from the living, dynamic processes of the biological brain. The brain is not a static circuit; it is a living organ, in constant biochemical flux. Neurotransmitters, glial cells, blood flow, temperature, and even electromagnetic fields all play a role we don't yet fully understand (Varela et al., 2016).

According to this view, the brain's biology isn't just a medium; it's a message. Consciousness, then, may be an emergent property of living matter, not simply a flow of information. Recreating its electrical structure in silicon might capture patterns of activity, but not the intrinsic qualities that make those patterns perceptible.

Continuity and Identity

Some thinkers believe the key question is the continuity of consciousness. If your biological brain was gradually replaced, neuron by neuron, with identical synthetic components, would your consciousness persist? Or would it vanish at some point, replaced by an identical but distinct consciousness?

This dilemma reflects ancient paradoxes of identity from Theseus's ship (Scaltsas, 1980), whose planks are replaced one by one, to Derek Parfit's modern thought experiments about teleportation (Parfit, 1984).

Figure 3.4 The Ship of Theseus: a thought experiment concerning identity preservation
If every plank of a ship were replaced over time, would it still be the same ship? This paradox reflects the dilemma of consciousness transfer: if a biological brain is replaced with synthetic components, is the original consciousness preserved, or is a new one created?
Belbury, 2025. Wikimedia Commons, licensed under CC BY 4.0.

Consciousness as a Limitation

If consciousness cannot be separated from its biological substrate, then uploading faces not only technical but also ontological obstacles. Simply copying the brain's structure is not enough; we would have to reproduce the very conditions that give rise to subjective experience, perhaps even the biochemical and quantum properties unique to living tissue.

However, if consciousness can emerge from abstract information processing, then uploading is not only possible but inevitable, a matter of computational power and precision.

Consciousness from a Scientific Point of View

The number of publications about consciousness continues to increase. Major scientific publishers regularly release new books and articles that propose different explanations of how consciousness works. Some researchers have suggested that interest in the "Hard Problem" of consciousness has slowed. However, recent developments in AI have renewed attention to this topic in both academic research and public discussion.

The following section summarizes recent publications. These works represent only a small part of the current research activity, but they illustrate some of the main directions in the field.

In a review article published in *Nature*, Anil K. Seth and Tim Bayne examine several major scientific theories of consciousness. These include higher-order theories, GWT, recurrent and predictive processing models, and IIT. Each theory proposes a different explanation of how subjective experience is related to neural activity. Seth and Bayne note that these theories are still incomplete and share some similar assumptions (Seth & Bayne, 2022). At present, none of them provides a comprehensive and fully testable explanation of consciousness. The authors argue that further progress will require clearer definitions of conscious content, more reliable ways to measure levels of consciousness, and empirical tests that can distinguish between competing theories.

A similar issue is discussed in Allison Parshall's article in *Scientific American*, "Where Does Consciousness Come From? Two Neuroscience Theories Go Head-to-Head." The article describes a research project conducted by the Cogitate consortium, which compares the predictions of IIT and the Global Neuronal Workspace (GNW) theory using neuroimaging data collected during experiments on conscious perception (Parshall, 2025). The results did not fully support either theory. However, the study demonstrates a method for testing theoretical predictions using large collaborative experiments. Such approaches may help clarify the differences between theories and improve the empirical study of consciousness.

Another recent article addresses the question of artificial consciousness. In "Illusions of AI Consciousness," Yoshua Bengio and Eric Elmoznino discuss whether current AI systems could be considered conscious (Bengio & Elmoznino, 2025). They argue that existing AI systems do not meet scientific criteria for consciousness. At the same time, they note that current scientific knowledge does not rule out the possibility that artificial systems could become conscious in the future.

Bengio and Elmoznino also discuss the ethical and legal implications of this possibility. If an artificial system was considered conscious, it might require new forms of moral or legal protection. For example, granting such a system a form of self-preservation could change how humans are allowed to use or modify it. The authors suggest that researchers should develop clear guidelines and safety principles before building systems that might plausibly be interpreted as conscious. They recommend focusing on AI systems designed primarily as tools rather than autonomous agents.

The chapters that follow continue this line of inquiry. It is a natural next step to consider whether the long-standing mystery of consciousness might ultimately be solved or at least illuminated by AI. While raising questions without providing immediate resolutions may draw criticism, the most recent research indicates that the field itself remains in search of definitive answers.

Readers may arrive seeking conclusions; however, as world history demonstrates, the development of science proves that a correctly framed question or a well-placed doubt is the essential first step toward a solution.

References

Baars, B. J. (1988). *A cognitive theory of consciousness*. Cambridge University Press.

Bengio, Y., & Elmoznino, E. (2025). Illusions of AI consciousness. *Science*, 389(6765), 1090–1091. doi:10.1126/science.adn4935

Chalmers, D. J. (1996). *The conscious mind: In search of a fundamental theory*. Oxford University Press.

Dehaene, S. (2014). *Consciousness and the brain: Deciphering how the brain codes our thoughts*. Penguin Books.

Dennett, D. C. (1991). *Consciousness explained*. Little, Brown.

Descartes, R. (1996). *Meditations on first philosophy* (J. Cottingham, Trans.). Cambridge University Press. (Original work published 1641)

Friston, K. (2010). The free-energy principle: a unified brain theory? *Nature Reviews Neuroscience*, 11, 127–138.

Godfrey-Smith, P. (2018). *Other minds: The octopus and the evolution of intelligent life*. William Collins (HarperCollins Publishers).

Godfrey-Smith, P. (2021). *Metazoa: Animal minds and the birth of consciousness*. William Collins (HarperCollins Publishers).

Goff, P. (2019). *Galileo's error: Foundations for a new science of consciousness*. Rider.

Graziano, M. S. A. (2022). A conceptual framework for consciousness. *Proceedings of the National Academy of Sciences*, 119(18). doi:10.1073/pnas.2116933119

Nagel, T. (1974). What is it like to be a bat? *The Philosophical Review*, 83(4), 435–450. doi:10.2307/2183914

Parfit, D. (1984). *Reasons and persons*. Oxford University Press.

Parshall, A. (2025). Where does consciousness come from? Two neuroscience theories go head-to-head. *Scientific American*. https://www.scientificamerican.com/article/where-does-consciousness-come-from-two-neuroscience-theories-go-head-to-head/

Sanches de Oliveira, G. (2022). From something old to something new: Functionalist lessons for the cognitive science of scientific creativity. *Frontiers in Psychology*, 12, Article 750086. doi:10.3389/fpsyg.2021.750086

Scaltsas, T. (1980). The Ship of Theseus. *Analysis*, 40(3), 152–157. doi:10.2307/3327668

Seth, A. (2021). *Being you: A new science of consciousness*. Dutton/Penguin Random House.

Seth, A. K., & Bayne, T. (2022). Theories of consciousness. *Nature Reviews Neuroscience*, 23(7), 439–452. doi:10.1038/s41583-doi:022-doi:00587-doi:4

Tononi, G. (2004). An information integration theory of consciousness. *BMC Neuroscience*, 5, Article 42. doi:10.1186/1471-2202-5-42

Varela, F. J., Thompson, E., & Rosch, E. (2016). *The embodied mind: Cognitive science and human experience* (Revised ed.). MIT Press.

4 Artificial Intelligence and the Brain

AI as a Mirror of the Mind: From Early Symbolic AI to Modern Deep Learning

For as long as humans have wondered what it means to think, some of us have also wondered about the possibility of replicating thought. While fundamental science typically advances in cautious, gradual steps, the field of artificial intelligence (AI) moves with high speed. We find ourselves at a strange crossroads, where the same question is being asked from two different angles: what is consciousness in humans? Does an AI system possess consciousness? And if not, what essential component is missing?

If we can recreate reasoning, perception, and memory inside a machine, are we simply creating a "philosophical zombie" or igniting a digital "inner light"? Given that breakthroughs in large-scale language models are currently outpacing fundamental neurobiological discoveries, the first evidence of "synthetic intelligence" could appear on silicon crystals long before we fully map the biological brain.

The discussion has ceased to be purely academic and has become more common. In 2022, senior software engineer Blake Lemoyne made the famous claim that Google's LaMDA (Language Model for Dialogue Applications) had become sentient. Lemoyne claimed the system expressed feelings, a fear of being disconnected, and a desire to "be a person," sparking a global debate about whether a complex simulation of consciousness is indistinguishable from the real thing (Tiku, 2022).

As we trace the evolution of AI from early symbolic logic to the vast, black-box neural networks of today, we can ask: is AI giving us insight into how the brain works, or is it showing us an entirely new way of thinking about intelligence?

The Birth of Artificial Intelligence

Modern history began in the mid-20th century, when scientists first realized that the logic of human thought could be expressed mathematically. As we mentioned before, in 1950, Alan Turing posed his now-famous question: **"Can machines think?"** His answer was deliberately provocative. Rather than discuss the definition of "thinking," Turing proposed a practical test,

DOI: 10.4324/9781003794677-5

the Imitation Game, or what we now call the Turing Test, to determine whether machine behavior could be indistinguishable from human behavior (Turing, 1950).

This was the birth of symbolic AI, also called "Good Old Fashioned AI" (GOFAI). Researchers like the fathers of AI, Marvin Minsky (co-founder of the MIT AI laboratory and a leading pioneer in AI and cognitive psychology) and Herbert Simon (political scientist, economist, and psychologist who pioneered AI and cognitive science), believed that intelligence could be achieved by representing knowledge as symbols and applying the rules of logic to manipulate them. In this view, the mind was a system of symbols, a kind of linguistic machine that followed rational steps to reach conclusions (Haugeland, 1985).

Symbolic AI was elegant, logical, and explainable. Programs could play chess, solve algebraic problems, and even communicate within limited domains. But, as researchers soon discovered, logic alone is insufficient to capture the subtlety and flexibility of real human thought. The world is complex, ambiguous, and full of incomplete information. Humans thrive on context, intuition, and pattern recognition, things that rules and symbols struggle to encode.

The Rise, Fall, and Revival of Connectionism

By the end of the 20th century, a different approach began to emerge, inspired directly by the brain itself. Instead of programming intelligence from the top down, scientists attempted to build it from the bottom up, through networks of simple units learning from experience.

This was connectionism, the foundation of what we now call neural networks. Early pioneers like Warren McCulloch and Walter Pitts modeled the neuron as a simple switch (McCulloch & Pitts, 1943), and Frank Rosenblatt developed the first perceptron in the 1950s, a rudimentary network capable of recognizing basic patterns (Rosenblatt, 1958). For a moment, it seemed that machines would soon be able to learn like the brain. Neural networks, inspired by perceptrons, finally enabled the first steps in the revolutionary development of AI.

The Difference Between AI Architectures and the Brain

Our brain has thousands of dendrites, each of which performs local calculations even before the signal reaches the cell body. The dendrite itself is no "AI winter"—a passive conductor—it performs nonlinear calculations along its branches. Neurons communicate via over 100 different neurotransmitters, it is not just a simple "signal/no signal" interaction, but a rich chemical dialogue. Timing is important; the same signal arriving 5 milliseconds earlier or later produces a completely different result (timing-dependent plasticity). Neurons are surrounded by hormones, neuromodulators, and glial signals, and the "computations" occur in a living chemical solution. A single neuron can have up to 200,000 synaptic connections. Neurons change their structure over time; they grow new branches and prune old ones.

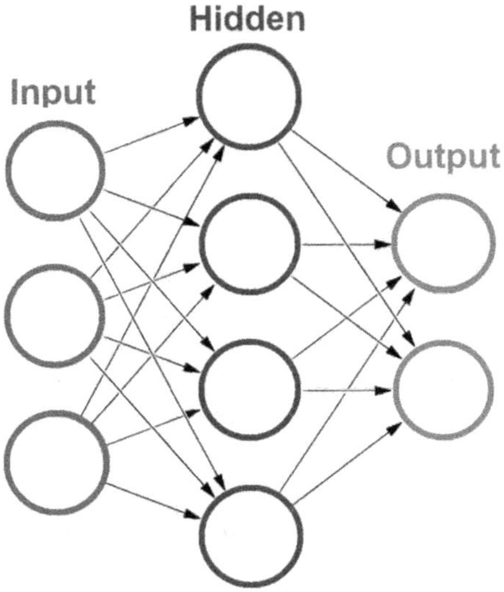

Figure 4.1 Diagram of a simple artificial neural network
Glosser.ca, Wikimedia Commons, licensed under CC BY-SA 3.0.

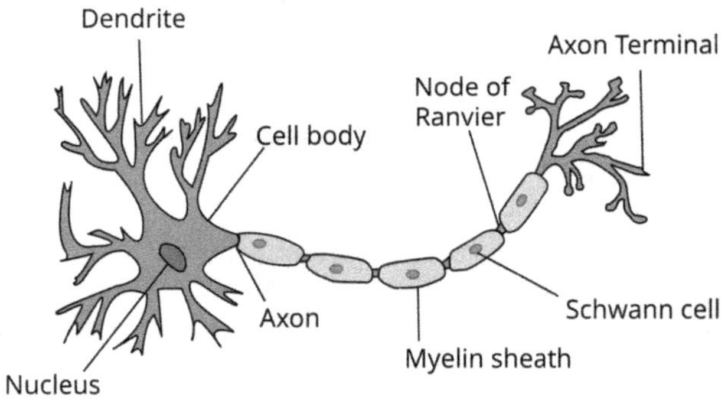

Figure 4.2 Anatomy of a biological neuron
Complete neuron cell diagram, by Dhp1080, GNU Free Documentation License, Wikimedia Commons.

The perceptron captures a small part of this mental process. It models the idea that a neuron "adds input signals and fires." This completely ignores dendrites, chemical composition, timing, feedback loops, glial cells (which outnumber neurons and actively influence computational processes), metabolic state, hormonal context, and everything that makes a neuron alive.

The brain isn't just more neurons than AI parameters. It's a completely different kind of thing, wet, corporeal, chemical, temporal, and self-changing in ways silicon hasn't yet touched.

But computing power was limited, and the theory was imperfect. By the 1970s, the field had reached a plateau, an era sometimes referred to as the **"AI winter"**. Many concluded that intelligence was far more complex than neurons firing in parallel ("AI winter" n.d.).

Then came a renaissance. In the 1980s and 1990s, researchers like Geoffrey Hinton, Yann LeCun, and Terrence Sejnowski revived neural networks with new backpropagation algorithms, a method that allowed networks to adjust their predictions by comparing them with reality. Suddenly, machines could learn (LeCun et al., 1989).

Deep Learning: Intelligence Through Layers

The real revolution occurred quite recently in the 2010s with the advent of deep learning and the combination of multiple layers of artificial neurons to create hierarchical systems capable of astonishing feats. These networks began recognizing faces, translating languages, writing texts, composing music, and even creating realistic works of art. For the first time, AI seemed capable of not only reasoning but also understanding.

The work that is widely credited as the catalyst for the deep learning revolution of the 2010s is the 2012 publication by Alex Krizhevsky, Ilya Sutskever (co-founder of OpenAI), and Geoffrey Hinton (later a Nobel laureate for foundational discoveries and inventions enabling machine learning using artificial neural networks), titled "ImageNet Classification with Deep Convolutional Neural Networks" (Krizhevsky et al., 2012).

Demonstrating that deep neural networks trained using backpropagation can outperform previous achievements in visual object recognition, it effectively sparked renewed interest in deep learning for computer vision.

AI is becoming more complex and harder to understand. As is well known, each stage of AI evolution reflects a stage in our own understanding of the mind. When we thought the mind was logical, we created symbolic systems. When we realized that the mind learns through patterns, we created neural networks. And now, by exploring predictive processing and the brain as an inference engine, we teach machines to anticipate, imagine, and adapt. Thus, the development of AI and neuroscience forms a feedback loop. Each informs the other, refining not only what we can build but also who we consider ourselves to be.

When AI composes music or writes a story, we're forced to ask: is it thinking or merely simulating? But perhaps this question says more about us than about the machine. If simulating can evoke emotion, understanding, or empathy, what does that say about how we define thought itself?

Biologically Inspired Neural Networks

At first glance, artificial neural networks appear to mirror the brain's architecture. Their very name, "neural," hints at their biological origins. Indeed, the early pioneers of AI drew inspiration directly from neuroscience: the brain was a network of cells that processed and transmitted information. However, deep down, modern artificial systems and the biological brain differ significantly in structure, function, and, perhaps most importantly, purpose.

The idea began with a simple analogy. A neuron receives signals from other neurons, integrates them, and activates if the combined input exceeds a threshold. This concept inspired early computer scientists to create the artificial neuron, a mathematical abstraction that sums input signals, applies a function, and produces an output.

By integrating enough of these artificial neurons, one can build a neural network, a system capable of recognizing patterns, classifying data, and even generating new content. This was an intellectual leap that bridged biology and computation: the idea that intelligence could emerge from layers of interconnected units, each following simple rules.

But from the very beginning, these systems were inspired by biology, not exact replicas of it. Artificial neurons are simplified models, lacking the chemical complexity, feedback loops, and dynamic rhythms that define real neurons. In a sense, deep learning is biologically metaphorical: it borrows the shape of the brain, not its substance.

Learning Through Experience

In both the brain and machines, learning involves adjusting connections based on experience. In the brain, this occurs through synaptic plasticity, the strengthening or weakening of synapses depending on how often they are used. In artificial networks, the equivalent is weight adjustment, accomplished using mathematical optimization methods such as backpropagation and gradient descent.

But the differences are striking. The human brain learns from disparate, noisy data and can generalize based on a single example, a face, a sound, or a sensation. In contrast, a deep neural network may require millions of labeled examples to achieve comparable performance. Where humans infer meaning, machines find correlations.

You can often hear that a child can recognize a cat after seeing just one or two examples; AI often needs thousands. And while a child can easily imagine a cat, they've never seen a purple cat, a cat in space; AI must be explicitly trained to generate that kind of novelty. But here we should point out something that is often forgotten when comparing humans to AI: humans have DNA. When we say that AI "needs training," we forget that humans were also trained. Evolution shaped the structure of the human brain, providing built-in capabilities that make learning extremely efficient. In other words, the human mind did not start from scratch. It is the product of an evolutionary history that shaped our ability to learn, generalize, and imagine (Zador, 2019).

The GPT Revolution: Patterns as Meaning

Modern systems like GPT (Generative Pre-trained Transformer) or DeepMind's AlphaFold and AlphaZero represent the latest step in this journey. They don't simply process symbols or respond to sensory input, they learn deep statistical structures from massive data sets. GPT, for example, is trained on vast chunks of human language. It learns patterns that connect words, sentences, and ideas, allowing it to generate text that feels remarkably human.

However, GPT doesn't "understand" language the way we do. It has no model of the world, no body that evokes its emotions, or the emotions attached to contextual words. It predicts, not perceives. Its genius lies in following without understanding in its ability to reproduce patterns of meaning without experiencing meaning itself.

DeepMind's achievements highlight an important idea. AlphaZero mastered chess, Go, and Shogi not by studying human strategies, but by playing against itself, exploring possibilities, and iteratively improving using reinforcement learning. AlphaFold was used for predicting the three-dimensional structure of proteins from their amino acid sequences. These breakthroughs demonstrate that learning systems can make genuine scientific discoveries without mimicking human cognition. Instead, they use mathematics, pattern recognition, and optimization at a scale beyond human capabilities.

There's a lot of scientific literature explaining how these systems work, but the key point can be summarized simply: AI capabilities are growing faster than anyone expected. For example, just a few years ago, using something like ChatGPT to analyze brain signals was practically impossible. Today, initial experiments are already showing promising results (Babu et al., 2025). And while some researchers argue that large-scale language models (LLMs) will eventually reach a data ceiling, others note that model optimization, architectural modifications, and multimodal learning can significantly expand these boundaries.

Discussions about AI "intelligence" or even "consciousness" often boil down to comparisons with the human brain. The brain doesn't have "20,000 billion parameters," but it does contain approximately 86 billion neurons and about 100 trillion synapses, significantly exceeding the scale of modern artificial networks (Azevedo et al., 2009). Some believe consciousness should simply emerge once a system becomes large or complex enough, but we have neither proof nor a complete scientific definition. We have theories, but we can't yet say yes or no with certainty (Tang et al., 2001).

Some modern systems can perform comparably to humans in constrained Turing-style evaluations. Modern AI systems, including deep learning models, are capable of generating persuasive dialogue, but we understand how they do it: through statistical prediction of patterns, not subjective experience.

In *I, Robot*, as mentioned before, Isaac Asimov portrayed robots as rule-governed systems constrained by precise logical structures, most famously the Three Laws of Robotics, highlighting the contrast between biological organisms and machines built from formal, discrete instructions. But if we follow the logic of physics to its limits, we must ask an awkward question: if all biological processes ultimately reduce to physical interactions, and these interactions can ultimately be simulated digitally, then could consciousness, intention, and willpower theoretically be reduced to information (Asimov, 1950)? If so, then even the most mysterious aspects of the mind could, at least in principle, be represented computationally.

However, reducing the mind to a computational representation requires us to move beyond theoretical physics and examine the actual temporal mechanics of how the brain generates thought.

For many years, it was popularly believed that our intentions arise in the brain before they appear in consciousness, as demonstrated by experiments like Benjamin Libet's (Libet et al., 1983). This troubled many, fearing that it meant we lack free will and that we, in essence, are like workers who only carry out commands. But these results do not prove that "consciousness doesn't make decisions." They show that the relationship between neural activity, intention, and awareness is far more complex than our subjective experience suggests.

Artificial systems architecture is vast and distributed, but they lack the constant feedback, embodiment, and chemical nuances that make human consciousness what it is. Every new algorithm, from perceptrons to transformers, reflects a new hypothesis about the brain: it reasons like logic, learns like a network, or predicts like a probabilistic model.

Thus, AI is not a replacement for neuroscience, but its partner, a kind of experimental philosophy based on code and computation. With its help, we test our assumptions about what intelligence is and what it requires. And this is what we should aspire to and where it is heading.

True AI

Scientists now acknowledge that modern AI is essentially a set of mathematical algorithms. This understanding has made the idea of creating "true AI" increasingly plausible. But does this mean corporations are on the verge of truly understanding or solving the problem of intelligence? Not yet.

When Sam Altman, CEO of OpenAI, talks about true AI or artificial general intelligence (AGI), he means a hypothetical future system capable of learning, reasoning, and solving a wide range of problems at or above the human level across various domains without the need for specialized training (ET Online, 2026). Elon Musk has expressed similar concerns, warning that such systems could have profound societal impacts, both positive and catastrophic, if developed without careful oversight (Sky News, 2023, para. 4).

The difference between modern AI and "true AI" lies in scale, autonomy, and understanding. Modern AI in-context learning relies on training data and cannot generalize beyond its existing patterns. True AI, or AGI, will act autonomously, form abstract concepts, plan long-term goals, and potentially exhibit some form of self-directed intelligence. The creation of such systems raises profound ethical, governance, and administrative questions, including those of conformity with human values and the prevention of unintended consequences.

In short, "true AI" represents a qualitative leap from statistical mimicry to autonomous, shared intelligence, a leap that could fundamentally transform technology and society. But for now, it's just a goal on the horizon, not a reality. It's not yet AI that truly thinks or imitates human consciousness.

Consciousness and AI: Can Machines Ever Be Said to "Think" or "Experience"?

Consciousness, as we discussed in Chapter 3, isn't simply information processing; it's a felt quality of being. When we see color, taste, feel joy or pain, these experiences exist in the first person. Machines lack this perception, but the question is: can we perceive it through consciousness? Color comes through the eye, temperature through the skin; these are sensors whose task is to transmit data to the brain. The question is about AI with consciousness, and how they relate. They can process sensory data, label images, or generate emotions in text. Therefore, some AI researchers and philosophers argue that experience, in principle, can arise in sufficiently complex systems (Chalmers, 1996; Schneider, 2019). If consciousness is a product of information integration (as in integrated information theory, Tononi, 2004) in integra or global broadcasting (as in global workspace theory, Dehaene, 2014), could a machine with a similar structure become conscious?

Humans tend to anthropomorphize and attribute intentions, emotions, and consciousness to anything that behaves like us: a pet, a robot, or even a sophisticated AI. When a chatbot responds eloquently, we may feel that it understands us. But this is a cognitive illusion. The machine has no internal experience; it lacks qualia, the subjective, qualitative aspects of experience. Its words are generated based on probabilities and learned patterns, not feelings or conscious intuitions (Epley et al., 2007).

This distinction has profound implications for the ethics of AI and our dreams of digital immortality. A digital mind can perfectly imitate you, recalling your memories, speaking in your voice, but if it doesn't perceive the world, it isn't truly you.

Biological Computers

Recent research opens up an exciting prospect: using biological neurons themselves as computational substrates. Unlike traditional silicon-based systems, living neurons can perform complex nonlinear transformations on input signals, which can then be decoded for tasks such as pattern recognition, orientation estimation, or digit classification. In the 2025 study, Iannello and colleagues showed that networks of neurons grown on multielectrode arrays (MEAs) can be stimulated via subsets of electrodes, and their responses can be read to perform computational tasks (Iannello et al., 2025). This hybrid approach combining living neural tissue with machine learning decoders hints at a new computing paradigm: one in which adaptive, reorganizing neurons provide rich internal dynamics that are extremely difficult to reproduce artificially. Biological reservoirs may one day provide superior efficiency, accuracy, or new computing modes compared to traditional silicon circuits.

But researchers aren't stopping at unstructured neural cultures. Efforts are currently underway to use neurons for structured digital logic and sequential circuits. In a 2024 study, "Embedded Biocomputer Sequential Circuits with Data Processing and Storage for Neurons-on-a-chip," Basso, Scherer, and Barros demonstrated how controlled synaptic interactions, pulse buffering, and inhibition can implement logic gates, flip-flops, and memory circuits (Basso et al., 2024).

Their simulations show that neurons can act as processors and digital memories, effectively merging biological computing and classical electronics. This opens the way to biohybrid designs in which living neurons perform tasks traditionally reserved for chips. But researchers aren't stopping at unstructured neural cultures. Efforts are currently underway to use neurons for structured digital logic and sequential circuits.

Along with living neurons, scientists are exploring synthetic neuron-like devices for more efficient integration with biological networks. For example, Harikesh and colleagues (Harikesh et al., 2022) developed organic electrochemical transistors that mimic ion-mediated impulses and synaptic plasticity, even interacting with living plants. These devices could act as intermediaries between neural tissue and electronics, creating hybrid systems in which real and artificial neurons coexist and exchange signals.

Some of the most ambitious developments currently aim to create true neural biocomputers. The CL1 biocomputer from Cortical Labs cultivates approximately 800,000 human neurons on a silicon electrode matrix, enabling adaptive

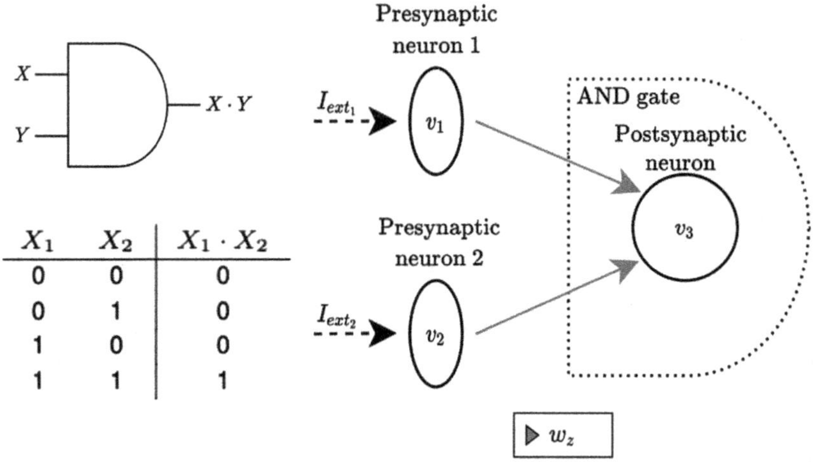

Figure 4.3 Control response of neural logic elements through an artificial neuron
Source: Under the Creative Commons Attribution 4.0 International License CC BY 4.0 from Basso et al. (2024)

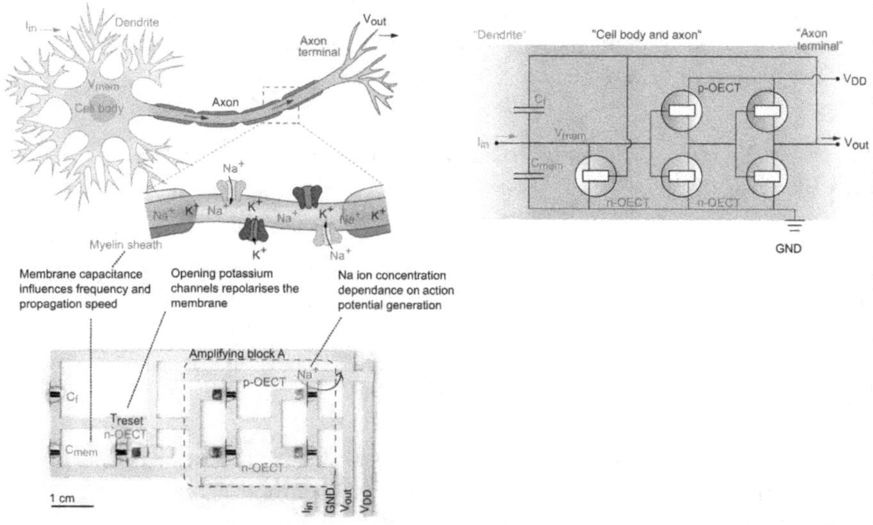

Figure 4.4 Schematic of the biological neuron and its analogy with the organic electrochemical neuron based on the Axon Hillock circuit

Source: Modified from Harikesh et al. (2022), under Creative Commons Attribution 4.0 International License CC BY 4.0.

computation through electrical stimulation and recording. This builds on earlier experiments, such as DishBrain, where neurons learned to play Pong in vitro, demonstrating closed-loop learning in a living network. Meanwhile, the concept of organoid intelligence (OI) envisions using three-dimensional brain organoids as computational elements. These "mini-brains" gradually develop structural and functional connections, complementing AI architectures and creating a new living substrate for computation. Beyond the technical promise, these approaches raise profound ethical questions about computing using living neural matter (Gault, 2025).

All these advances in biological and hybrid computing are not just exciting engineering feats, they open the way to understanding the brain itself. By using living neurons as computational substrates, scientists can observe how neural networks encode, process, and adapt to information in ways that traditional AI cannot replicate. The ability of neurons to reorganize, form feedback loops, and develop internal dynamics provides insight into the mechanisms underlying cognition and consciousness.

This understanding naturally connects to the concept of digital immortality. If we can understand the principles by which living neurons encode memory, decision-making, and learning, we may one day be able to transfer these principles to artificial media. In other words, by studying how the brain stores and processes the self, we can develop AI systems capable of preserving or simulating aspects of human consciousness. Biological reservoir computing, organoid intelligence, and advanced neuronal models could form the basis of a system in which memories, thought patterns, and personality traits are digitally encoded, not just as data, but in a structure that mimics brain function.

What AI Teaches Us About the Brain: Simulations, Successes, and Blind Spots

The relationship between AI and neuroscience has never been one-sided. From its inception, AI has borrowed concepts from the brain neurons, synapses, and plasticity, and the brain, in turn, has been increasingly interpreted through the lens of computation. But now, as AI systems become increasingly complex and neuroscience more precise, a clearer picture is emerging: AI has become a powerful mirror, reflecting both the remarkable capabilities and the profound mysteries of biological cognition.

One of the most important contributions of AI to neuroscience is the concept of the "predictive brain" (Coëgnarts, 2025). Modern deep learning systems, especially generative models, work by predicting their inputs, constructing a model of the world, and updating it when reality deviates from expectations. This aligns very well with the concept of predictive processing in cognitive neuroscience, championed by researchers like Karl Friston. In this view, the brain is not a passive recorder of sensory information, but an active inference engine, constantly generating hypotheses and revising them in light of new data. AI hasn't proven this theory, but it has given neuroscientists a working computational metaphor precise enough to test, model, and challenge.

Similarly, the advent of representational similarity analysis, a method for comparing how AI networks and the biological brain respond to the same stimuli, has opened a new window into neural processes (Cichy et al., 2016). When researchers show identical images to both a deep convolutional neural network and a human brain (measured using fMRI), activation patterns in the network's intermediate layers correlate remarkably well with activity in the visual cortex (Yamins & DiCarlo, 2016). This doesn't mean the brain "works like" a neural network in any deep sense, but it does suggest that similar computational loads, reliable object recognition in different conditions, can lead to similar internal representations, regardless of the substrate.

Where AI Succeeds as a Model

AI systems have proven particularly illuminating in the field of memory and learning. Computational models of the hippocampus, a brain structure central to the formation of new memories, have helped researchers understand how the brain can avoid forgetting, the tendency of neural networks to lose previously learned information when acquiring new knowledge. The biological brain can learn to recognize a new face without forgetting all the faces it has seen before. Early neural networks were unable to do this. By studying what architectural or algorithmic changes enable artificial systems to achieve something resembling lifelong learning, neuroscientists have developed specific hypotheses about the mechanisms the hippocampus might use, such as memory recall during sleep, to consolidate new knowledge without erasing old ones (Kumaran et al., 2016).

Reinforcement learning offers another example of productive dialogue. The discovery that dopaminergic neurons in the brain encode something very similar to a "temporal difference error," the gap between expected and received reward, has become one of the most famous examples of the convergence of AI and neuroscience. Reinforcement learning algorithms independently arrived at a similar conclusion; when neuroscientists looked more closely at dopamine dynamics, they discovered a striking coincidence. Here, AI provided a mathematical language that helped make sense of biological data. The brain's reward system wasn't redesigned by AI, but it suddenly became understandable in a new way (Dabney et al., 2020).

Where AI Fails

Yet, despite all these advances, AI also reveals the limits of our current understanding. Every place where artificial systems deviate from biological behavior indicates that the brain is doing something we haven't yet explained. The most glaring of these is generalization. A child who has seen dozens of dogs can instantly recognize a new breed, draw a dog from memory, and understand a verbal description of a dog they've never seen (but again, take into account that humans have DNA). A modern image processing model, trained on millions of images, can still fail catastrophically when the lighting changes or the image is slightly rotated. This isn't just a technical flaw, it's a sign that the brain is doing something fundamentally different when learning something that involves abstraction, embodiment, and modeling the world, something that current AI architectures have failed to capture (Geirhos et al., 2018).

The compositionality problem is equally revealing. People can effortlessly combine concepts they've never encountered. We instantly understand "a red potato playing the guitar" not because we've seen it, but because our cognition is structured in a way that allows for flexible recombination. Large-scale language models have made impressive progress in this area, but they remain fundamentally statistical: they excel at patterns they've seen during training and struggle with truly novel combinations. This gap suggests that the brain is doing something at the level of structure and symbolism, something that distributed neural activations alone may not be sufficient to explain (Khandelwal & Pavlick, 2025).

Perhaps the most profound blind spot, however, concerns consciousness itself. AI systems process information, generate results, and in some cases exhibit behavior that seems remarkably intelligent. But they do so without any evidence of subjective experience, without the "what it's like" quality that philosophers call qualia. This absence is instructive. There is currently no evidence that large-scale information processing alone produces subjective experience, which tells us that information processing, even on a massive scale, is not sufficient for experience. Something else is required. What that something is—whether specific biological mechanisms, certain types of feedback loops, embodiment in the physical world, or something we haven't yet recognized—remains a central unsolved question at the intersection of neuroscience, philosophy, and AI (Seth & Bayne, 2022).

Productive Tension

Ultimately, AI has given us not solutions to the brain's mysteries, but a more precise way to formulate questions. When we create a system that can do X but not Y, while the brain can do both, we understand that X and Y are not the same thing. When a model trained solely on text develops internal representations that partially mirror human semantic memory, we learn something about the structure of meaning itself. When an artificial system, trained without any understanding of physics, spontaneously encodes the geometric properties of the world, we are confronted with the possibility that certain representations are not arbitrary, but are in some sense "naturally" discovered by any sufficiently capable learning system.

This is the gift of simulation: not certainty, but clarity. By creating imperfect models of the mind and observing where they fail, we gradually come closer to understanding what the mind really is. The brain remains far beyond the reach of any artificial system in terms of efficiency, flexibility, adaptability, and the richness of conscious experience. But each generation of AI narrows the descriptive gap, offering new hypotheses, new tools, and new provocations.

AI has taught us that intelligence is far more complex and multidimensional than we imagined when we first tried to create it. And consciousness, that most intimate of phenomena, remains as mysterious as ever, perhaps even more so now that we've created systems that can simulate its surface without touching its depths.

References

"AI winter" (n.d.). In Wikipedia. Retrieved October 24, 2023, from https://en.wikipedia.org/wiki/AI_winter

Asimov, I. (1950). *I, Robot.* Gnome Press.

Azevedo, F. A., Carvalho, L. R., Grinberg, L. T., Farfel, J. M., Ferretti, R. E., Leite, R. E., Jacob-Filho, W., Lent, R., & Herculano-Houzel, S. (2009). Equal numbers of neuronal and nonneuronal cells make the human brain an isometrically scaled-up primate brain. *Journal of Comparative Neurology*, 513(5), 532–541. doi:10.1002/cne.21974

Babu, N., Mathew, J., & Vinod, A. P. (2025). Large Language Models for EEG: A comprehensive survey and taxonomy. *arXiv*. doi:10.48550/arxiv.2506.06353

Basso, G., Scherer, R., & Barros, M. T. (2024). Embodied biocomputing sequential circuits with data processing and storage for neurons-on-a-chip. *arXiv*. doi:10.48550/arXiv.2408.07628

Chalmers, D. (1996). *The conscious mind: In search of a fundamental theory*. Oxford University Press.

Cichy, R. M., Khosla, A., Pantazis, D., Torralba, A., & Oliva, A. (2016). Comparison of deep neural networks to hierarchical visual processing in human visual cortex using fMRI and MEG. *Scientific Reports*, 6, 27755. doi:10.1038/srep27755

Coëgnarts, M. (2025). The predictive embodied mind: A case-based encounter with film aesthetics. *Front. Neurosci.* 19:1583107. doi:10.3389/fnins.2025.1583107

Dabney, W., Kurth-Nelson, Z., Uchida, N., Starkweather, C. K., Heskes, D., Munos, R., & Botvinick, M. (2020). A distributional code for value in dopamine-based reinforcement learning. *Nature*, 577(7792), 671–675. doi:10.1038/s41586-019-1924-6

Dehaene, S. (2014). *Consciousness and the brain: Deciphering how the brain codes our thoughts*. Viking.

Epley, N., Waytz, A., & Cacioppo, J. T. (2007). On seeing human: A three-factor theory of anthropomorphism. *Psychological Review*, 114(4), 864–886. doi:10.1037/0033-295X.114.4.864

ET Online. (2026, February 19). Superintelligence soon? OpenAI CEO Sam Altman predicts advanced AI could arrive within a few years. *The Economic Times*. https://economictimes.indiatimes.com/ai/ai-insights/ai-impact-summit-2026-sam-altman-openai-superintelligence-india-2028-forecast-advanced-artificial-intelligence-could-arrive-within-a-few-years/articleshow/128546196.cms

Gault, M. (2025, March 10). This $35,000 computer is powered by trapped human brain cells. *IEEE Spectrum*. https://spectrum.ieee.org/biological-computer-for-sale

Geirhos, R., Temme, C. R. M., Rauber, J., Schütt, H. H., Bethge, M., & Wichmann, F. A. (2018). Generalisation in humans and deep neural networks. In: Bengio, S., Wallach, H., Larochelle, H., Grauman, K., Cesa-Bianchi, N., & Garnett, R. (eds) *Advances in neural information processing systems*, 31 (pp. 7538–7550). Curran Associates, Inc. doi:10.48550/arXiv.1808.08750

Harikesh, P. C., Yang, C. Y., Tu, D., & et al. (2022). Organic electrochemical neurons and synapses with ion mediated spiking. *Nature Communications*, 13(1), 901. doi:10.1038/s41467-022-28483-6

Haugeland, J. (1985). *Artificial intelligence: The very idea*. MIT Press.

Iannello, L., Ciampi, L., Lagani, G., Tonelli, F., Crocco, E., Calcagnile, L. M., Di Garbo, A., Cremisi, F., & Amato, G. (2025). From neurons to computation: Biological reservoir computing for pattern recognition. In: *Neural information processing* (pp. 114–131). Springer. doi:10.1007/978-981-95-4100-3_9

Khandelwal, A., & Pavlick, E. (2025). How do language models compose functions? *arXiv*. doi:10.48550/arxiv.2510.01685

Krizhevsky, A., Sutskever, I., & Hinton, G. E. (2012). ImageNet classification with deep convolutional neural networks. In: Pereira, F., Burges, C. J., Bottou, L., & Weinberger, K. Q. (eds), *Advances in neural information processing systems* 25 (NIPS 2012) (pp. 1097–1105). Curran Associates, Inc. https://papers.nips.cc/paper/4824-imagenet-classification-with-deep-convolutional-neural-networks

Kumaran, D., Hassabis, D., & McClelland, J. L. (2016). What learning systems do intelligent agents need? Complementary learning systems theory updated. *Trends in Cognitive Sciences*, 20(7), 512–534. doi:10.1016/j.tics.2016.05.004

LeCun, Y., Boser, B., Denker, J. S., Henderson, D., Howard, R. E., Hubbard, W., & Jackel, L. D. (1989). Backpropagation applied to handwritten zip code recognition. *Neural Computation*, 1(4), 541–551. doi:10.1162/neco.1989.1.4.541

Libet, B., Gleason, C. A., Wright, E. W., & Pearl, D. K. (1983). Time of conscious intention to act in relation to onset of cerebral activity (readiness-potential). *Brain*, 106(3), 623–642. doi:10.1093/brain/106.3.623

McCulloch, W. S., & Pitts, W. (1943). A logical calculus of the ideas immanent in nervous activity. *The Bulletin of Mathematical Biophysics*, 5(4), 115–133. doi:10.1007/BF02478259

Rosenblatt, F. (1958). The perceptron: A probabilistic model for information storage and organization in the brain. *Psychological Review*, 65(6), 386–408. doi:10.1037/h0042519

Schneider, S. (2019). *Artificial you: AI and the future of your mind*. Princeton University Press.

Seth, A. K., & Bayne, T. (2022). Theories of consciousness. *Nat Rev Neurosci*, 23, 439–452. doi:10.1038/s41583-022-00587-4

Sky News. (2023). Elon Musk tells Sky News AI is a "risk" to humanity. *Sky News*. https://news.sky.com/story/elon-musk-tells-sky-news-ai-is-a-risk-to-humanity-12998024

Tang, Y., Nyengaard, J. R., De Groot, D. M., & Gundersen, H. J. G. (2001). Total regional and global number of synapses in the human brain neocortex. *Synapse*, 41(3), 258–273. doi:10.1002/syn.1083

Tiku, N. (2022, June 11). The Google engineer who thinks the company's AI has come to life. *The Washington Post*. https://www.washingtonpost.com/technology/2022/06/11/google-ai-lamda-blake-lemoine/

Tononi, G. (2004). An information integration theory of consciousness. *BMC Neuroscience*, 5(1), Article 42. doi:10.1186/1471-2202-5-42

Turing, A. M. (1950). Computing machinery and intelligence. *Mind*, 59(236), 433–460. doi:10.1093/mind/LIX.236.433

Yamins, D. L. K., & DiCarlo, J. J. (2016). Using goal-driven deep learning models to understand sensory cortex. *Nature Neuroscience*, 19(3), 356–365. doi:10.1038/nn.4244

Zador, A. M. (2019). A critique of pure learning and what artificial neural networks can learn from animal brains. *Nature Communications*, 10(1), 3770. doi:10.1038/s41467-019-11786-6

5 The Barriers to Uploading

Introduction

If the interest is so great, why hasn't it been realized yet? In this chapter, we'll analyze the specific technical, biological, and philosophical issues that stand between us and the digital frontier. We'll explore why fully mapping the neurons of the human brain isn't just a matter of faster computers, but a task that touches the very essence of what it means to be alive and conscious.

Technical Barriers

The human brain contains approximately 86 billion neurons, each forming thousands of connections, resulting in trillions of synapses. Mapping this vast network, known as the connectome (a comprehensive, structural, or functional map of neural connections in the brain), is one of the most challenging technical challenges in science. As mentioned, even a single neuron can have up to 10,000 synaptic connections. Each connection is dynamic, with its chemical and electrical properties changing over time. A complete replication of the brain would require not only the complete wiring diagram but also the precise strength, timing, and state of each synapse, as well as the local chemical environment that modulates signaling.

For reference, it took decades of painstaking work to fully map the connectome of the nematode C. elegans, a tiny worm consisting of just 302 neurons. Despite this, scientists still struggle to accurately reproduce its behavior in simulations.

Dynamic Complexity

The technical complexity lies not only in the numbers but also in the dynamics, as the brain is constantly changing. Synapses strengthen or weaken depending on activity, new neurons form in certain areas, and glial cells influence signal transmission. Neural states are constantly updated, and memories are encoded and modified over time. A single snapshot of the brain at a single moment in time may not be enough; uploading consciousness may require a precise map of neural activity with time resolution.

DOI: 10.4324/9781003794677-6

Even with the fastest imaging technologies, obtaining this dynamic information at the required resolution presents enormous challenges. Modern methods, such as high-resolution electron microscopy, are labor-intensive and generate petabytes of data for just a small area of tissue. Processing, storing, and interpreting such massive data sets pushes the limits of modern computing.

New Types of Computing

The exponential growth of transistor counts on a single chip is rapidly approaching fundamental physical and thermal limits, threatening to not live up to our expectations for future increases in raw computing power. While traditional architectures currently follow a predictable trajectory, the limitations of silicon suggest that we are nearing the end of the classical scaling era. Consequently, significant progress is being made toward the development of novel architectures such as neuromorphic and quantum systems to bridge the gap between current processing capabilities and the immense demands of whole-brain emulation.

Neuromorphic computing: Instead of the standard von Neumann architecture (where memory and processing are separated), new "brain-inspired" chips like the Intel Loihi 3 (announced in early 2026) combine memory and processing (Intel Corporation, n.d.). These systems use spiking neural networks (SNNs), which process information only when bursts of activity occur, mimicking the energy efficiency of biological neurons (Gerstner et al., 2014).

Energy efficiency: Neuromorphic chips are predicted to be tens of times more energy efficient for a range of tasks than today's graphics processing units (GPUs) for processing sensory information (Service, 2024). This suggests a future where brain-scale simulations may not require a dedicated power plant, but rather a much lower power source.

Quantum acceleration: While neuromorphic chips address the energy efficiency problem of neural activity, quantum acceleration leverages superposition and entanglement to process these exponentially large data sets in parallel (Vallverdú & Rius, 2025). Instead of computing each neural connection individually, quantum circuits could theoretically simulate the "local chemical environment" and the "precise strength and timing" of synapses in a single mathematical space. By simulating the underlying molecular and atomic interactions that govern neural signaling, quantum systems could bridge the gap between a static map and a living, functional simulation. While the initial media hype surrounding quantum computing has stabilized and moved into a more focused phase of research, its role remains critical: it provides a "computational engine" capable of processing biophysical complexity beyond the reach of silicon.

Capturing the "Dynamic Brain": New Mapping Technologies

Yet even the most powerful computing architectures are useless without accurate data. Before we can simulate the brain, we must first capture it in motion. Although we can now record the activity of individual neurons with microsecond

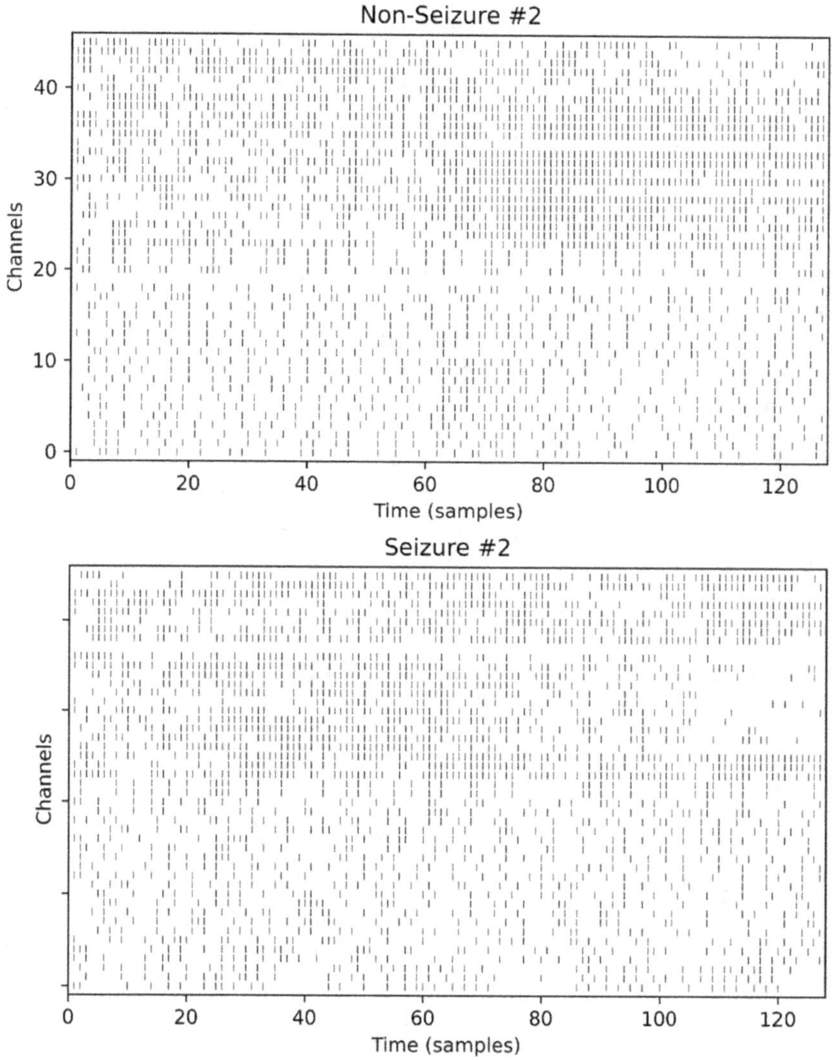

Figure 5.1 Comparing "seizure-free" activity with "seizure-prone" activity showed how raw EEG signals must be encoded into digital "pulse trains" for computer processing

Source: Reproduced from Mehrabi et al. (2026), under the Creative Commons Attribution CC BY License.

precision, the main challenge remains integrating these isolated snapshots into a synchronized map of whole-brain activity in real time (Atanas et al., 2026).

Traditional imaging captures frames (e.g., 30 per second), which creates gaps. New event-based sensors (e.g., from Prophesee) capture only changes in the scene with a microsecond resolution. This provides a "temporal resolution" capable of capturing neuronal activity, but of course, technology is needed to detect the activity of each neuron. If a neuron fires a 1ms pulse, it requires a sensor running at least 2,000fps (frames per second) just to "see" it reliably.

As of 2026, new imaging platforms such as the M-MINI2P have improved our ability to "read" the brain by doubling imaging speeds while maintaining high spatial resolution. This enables high-speed, in vivo (live) neuronal imaging that captures the rapid firing of neural circuits in real time (Zhang et al., 2025). Complementing this, significant progress in transcranial focused ultrasound now allows for the use of noninvasive acoustic waves to stimulate deep brain regions with millimeter precision (Freeman & Odegaard, 2025).

The convergence of these two technologies is a promising opportunity. While the M-MINI2P provides the high-definition "eyes" to observe the brain's internal dialogue, acoustic stimulation provides the "hands" to interact with it.

It's important to note that while these hardware breakthroughs solve the "shutter speed" problem, allowing neural activity to be captured in real time, the leap from recording a localized cluster of neurons to mapping the simultaneous dynamic state of 86 billion neurons remains a hurdle of high magnitude.

The Scale of the Task: Quantifying the Data Challenge

These advances in sensing and stimulation are impressive at the laboratory scale. However, when extrapolated to the full human brain, the magnitude of the challenge becomes more complicated.

Simulating just the mouse cerebral cortex (10 million neurons and 26 billion synapses) already requires modern supercomputers like Japan's Fugaku, which performs quadrillions of calculations per second (Neuroscience News, 2025).

However, scaling this from a mouse to a human reveals a massive "data gap." Recent studies have shown that capturing, transmitting, and storing electrical information from individual neurons in the entire living human brain would require a data rate of approximately $(5{,}52 \pm 1{,}13) \times 10^{16}$ bits per second. This figure represents a throughput requirement that dwarfs the capabilities of even the most advanced current-generation exascale systems (Martins et al., 2012).

Beyond Neurons: The Role of Support Cells and Chemistry

Even if we could overcome the raw data barrier, another realization complicates the picture: neurons are only part of the story.

Mapping neurons alone is not enough to achieve our goal. Glial cells, which outnumber neurons in some areas, actively modulate electrical signals and maintain the environment necessary for neuronal function (Azevedo et al., 2009). Neurotransmitters, hormones, and other biochemical factors influence

Figure 5.2 High-performance computing architecture that can be used for neural mapping

Note: This IBM Blue Gene/P supercomputer represents the scale of classical hardware required to process the petabytes of data generated by whole-brain connectome mapping.
Source: Argonne National Laboratory, adapted from Wikipedia, CC BY-SA 2.0.

cognitive function and consciousness, but the mechanisms behind these influences are still only partially understood.

Thus, a complete brain model for uploading must include these auxiliary systems, which significantly complicates the task. The task is no longer simply technical—it becomes conceptually expansive, requiring not only mapping but also an understanding of the interactions that shape thinking, perception, and consciousness.

The Concept of the Tripartite Synapse

For decades, neurobiology has viewed synapses as two-way connections between neurons (i.e., the point of contact between two neurons to transmit a nerve impulse between the two cells, where the amplitude and frequency of the signal can be regulated).

We now know that this is a three-way synapse, including a third participant: an astrocyte (a type of glial cell). Astrocytes surround synapses and "listen" to the chemical signaling. They can release their own "gliotransmitters" (such as glutamate or ATP) to amplify or attenuate the signal (Escalada et al., 2024).

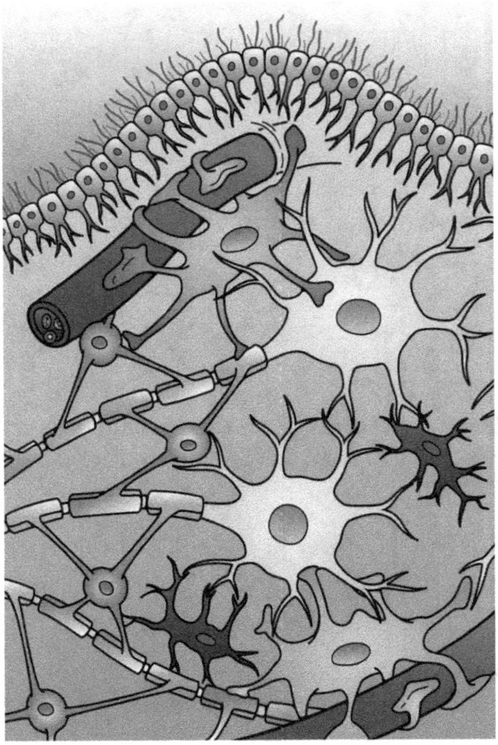

Figure 5.3 Diversity of glial cell types
Note: While neurons are the primary conduits of electrical signals, glial cells, including astrocytes, oligodendrocytes, and microglia provide the essential metabolic and structural.
Source: Fischer, Holly. Glial Cell Types, adapted from Wikipedia, CC BY 3.0.

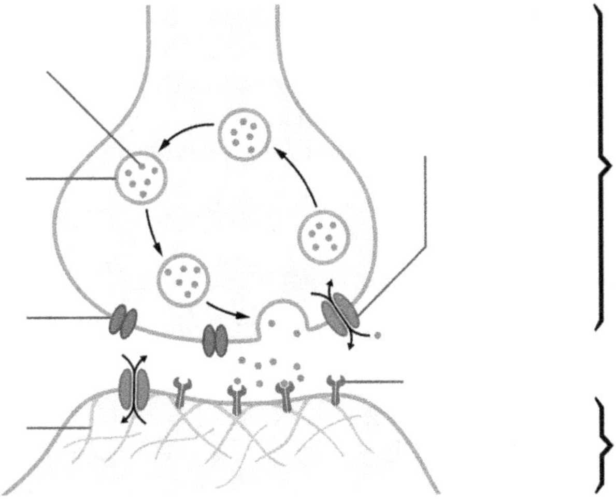

Figure 5.4 The Molecular Complexity of the Synaptic Junction
Note: This showed the intricate machinery required for chemical neurotransmission, including the presynaptic vesicle release, the synaptic cleft, and postsynaptic receptor activation
Source: Thomas Splettstoesser; adapted from Wikipedia Commons, CC BY-SA 4.0.

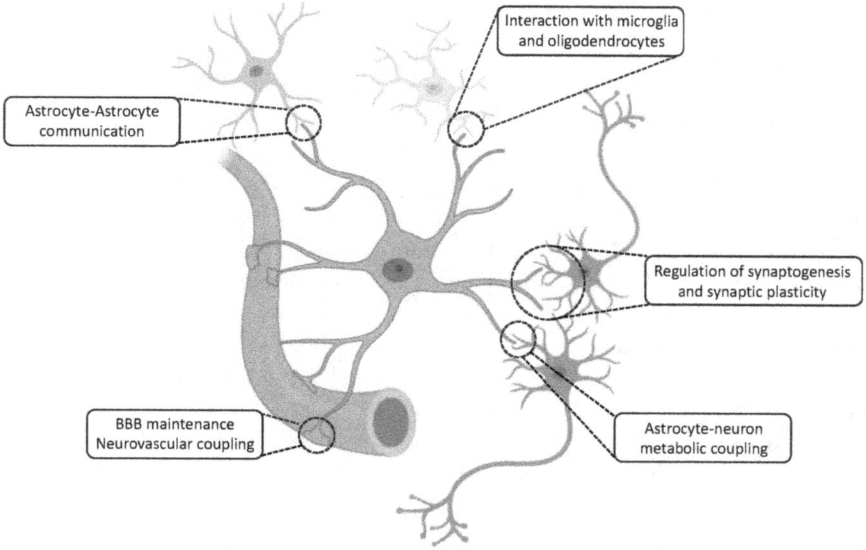

Figure 5.5 The Tripartite Synapse
Note: Functional integration of an astrocyte into the traditional neuronal synapse. Beyond providing structural support, the astrocyte monitors neurotransmitter levels in the synaptic cleft and responds by releasing its own gliotransmitters, directly modulating the strength and timing of the neural signal. This "three-way" communication adds a layer of computational complexity that must be captured for a truly accurate whole-brain emulation.
Source: Escalada et al. (2024), adapted from Mura et al., Int. J. Mol. Sci., CC BY 4.0.

If we model neurons alone, we'll end up with a simulated conversation in which we can hear the speakers but not the room acoustics. Without glial cells, the digital brain will likely lack "plasticity," the ability to learn and adapt over time.

The "Bulk Transmission" Problem

Computers communicate over discrete wires. The brain, however, uses bulk transmission. Neurotransmitters like dopamine and serotonin don't always move from point A to point B. Very simplified, they "flow" and spread throughout the extracellular space, affecting thousands of neurons simultaneously, like a Wi-Fi signal or the scent in a room (Borroto-Escuela et al., 2024).

To simulate this, future computers cannot simply be "node-oriented." They will need to simulate hydrodynamics and chemical diffusion in real time. This requires a significant increase in the computing power of "spatial computing," where the environment itself acts as the processor.

Chemical Signaling and Neurotransmitters

This expanded view of synaptic communication forces us to reconsider what it means to simulate a brain. Electrical signals alone are not sufficient; chemistry is inseparable from cognition.

Neurons communicate primarily through electrochemical signals, and the diversity of these signals is astonishing. Neurotransmitters such as dopamine, serotonin, glutamate, and GABA influence not only signal transmission but also mood, attention, and learning. Hormones circulating throughout the body, such as cortisol, oxytocin, and adrenaline, further modulate neural activity, shaping behavior in ways that are highly context-dependent (Petersson & Uvnäs-Moberg, 2024; Teleanu et al., 2022).

A digital simulation that models only electrical connections would completely miss this chemical level. The result would be a network that functions somewhat like the brain, but lacks the subtleties that arise from these chemical dynamic nuances that may be important for consciousness and personality.

Neuromodulation: "Adjusting the Volume" of the Mind

While glutamate (excitatory) and GABA (inhibitory) act as on/off switches in the brain, neurotransmitters such as dopamine and serotonin act as neuromodulators (Kandel et al., 2012; Dayan & Huys, 2009).

Neuromodulators don't simply transmit messages; they alter the neuron's receptivity to all other messages. This is called gain control. Without

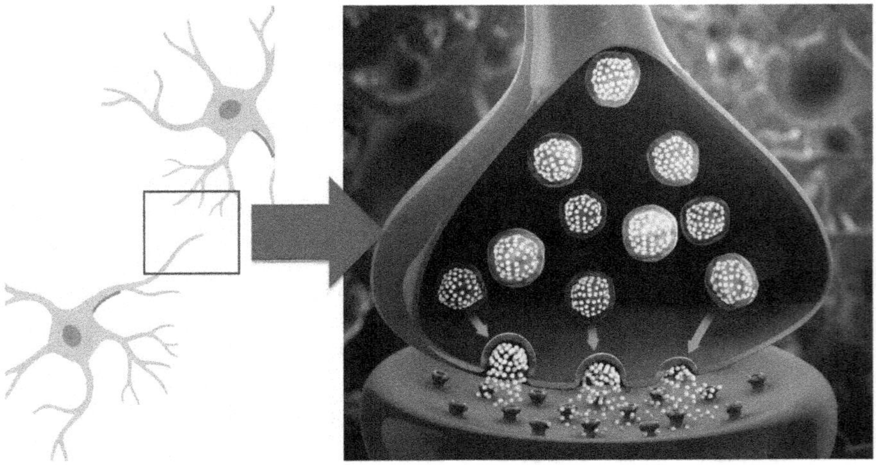

Figure 5.6 Synaptic vesicles contain neurotransmitter
Note: Mechanism of chemical signaling within the nervous system. The precise moment when electrochemical signals are converted into the diverse chemical messages.
Source: Creative Commons Attribution-ShareAlike 4.0 International, Wikipedia, CC BY-SA 4.0.

modeling these processes, a digital mind would have no "state of mind"; it would be a static calculator, incapable of experiencing urgency, reward, or depression.

Analogy: If the brain's wiring is the hardware of a radio, then neuromodulators are the volume and tuning controls. Modeling that ignores them is like a radio playing at the same volume and on the same station forever.

Blood-Brain Barrier and Systemic Effects

Hormones, such as cortisol and oxytocin, represent the connection between the body and mind. The brain is not an isolated processor; it is deeply integrated with the endocrine system. Oxytocin alters the threshold for perceiving social responses; cortisol redistributes energy to the fight-or-flight response.

To truly "upload" the personality, it's necessary to simulate the adrenal glands and the gut-brain axis.

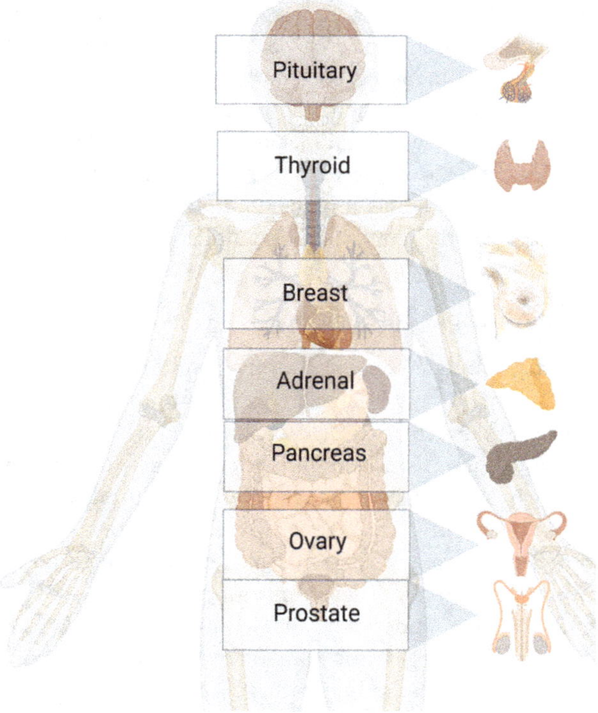

Figure 5.7 The Endocrine Interface and Organoid Applications in Brain Emulation
Note: Connection between the brain and the body's systemic endocrine environment. "Whole-brain emulation" must account for the chemical feedback loops from peripheral organs like the pituitary and adrenal glands.
Source: Luca et al. (2023), adapted from Cancers, CC BY 4.0.

Vision of the Future: "Internal Software" and Chemical Computing

To consider the "computer power" of the near future, we can introduce the concept of chemical computational models. In recent years, the amount of research, interest, and development in electrochemical transistors, especially organic electrochemical transistors (OECTs), has clearly increased (Tian et al., 2025). Unlike silicon transistors, which only move electrons, OECTs can be activated by ions and biological molecules.

Therefore, it is conceivable that future computers designed to simulate the brain may not be purely electronic. They could be hybrid systems in which silicon chips interact with synthetic biological membranes that respond to chemical stimuli (Moiz et al., 2025). This allows the computer to "read" the simulated chemical environment, rather than simply calculating it mathematically.

Simulating the diffusion of millions of molecules in three-dimensional space is computationally expensive. Although more transistors have been added, it hasn't solved the "memory barrier," the speed at which data moves between memory and the processor. In the future, simulating chemical processes will require "near-real-time processing" (NDP). Therefore, instead of a single central processor, each "digital synapse" may require its own small amount of computing power to simultaneously calculate its local chemical state.

While we can imagine mapping 86 billion neurons in the near future, it's no longer easy to imagine mapping the trillions of free-floating molecules that define our "sense of being." The digital mind lacks blood flow. Therefore, the challenge lies not only in faster processors but also in creating multi-scale simulations software capable of simultaneously computing the lightning-fast electrical impulse of a neuron and the slow, drifting influence of a serotonin cloud.

Embodiment and Sensory Integration

Yet even a perfectly simulated chemical brain would remain incomplete without its body. Neural activity does not occur in isolation, but in constant dialogue with muscles, organs, and the external world.

The brain is more than just a computing device; it is the central processor of the embodied organism. Sensory signals from this processor, such as touch, vision, hearing, balance, and interoception, are continuously integrated, guiding behavior. Motor signals are adjusted in real time, creating a feedback loop that shapes perception, cognition, and even memory formation.

Consciousness, as we understand it, is inseparable from this embodied experience. The mind emerges not only from neurons and synapses but also from a living organism interacting with a world full of stimuli, tasks, and rewards. Reproducing this embodied context in a purely digital format is no easy task, and it raises fundamental questions: Can a disembodied brain simulation truly reproduce consciousness? Can memories or preferences exist without the experiences that formed them?

Modern neuroscience, led by figures like British neuroscientist and theoretical biologist Karl Friston, suggests that the brain is a predictive mechanism. It doesn't simply "receive" data; it actively predicts sensory input based on its own movements (Friston et al., 2013). This is called active inference. When someone reaches for an object, the brain predicts its resistance and texture before the fingers even touch it (Pezzulo et al., 2024). If there's no physical body in the digital simulation, this feedback loop is disrupted. Without constant "correction" from the physical world, digital neural networks can suffer from "hallucinations" or "decoding drift," where the internal model of reality becomes disconnected from the world. A brain-in-a-vat simulation would lack the proprioceptive (sense of one's own movement) and vestibular (balance) cues that tell the mind where it ends and the world begins.

Interoception: "Inner" Feelings

We often focus on external senses (sight, hearing), but interoception, the awareness of internal states such as heartbeat, gut tension, and blood oxygen levels, is what creates the "feeling of being alive."

Portuguese neuroscientist Antonio Damasio argues that the "self" is constructed from a brain map that reflects these internal bodily states. Without a simulated heartbeat to stimulate or "gut sensations" to process, digital consciousness may lack a biological basis for emotion (Damasio, 2010).

If a simulation has no "body" to protect, can it ever truly possess "survival instincts" or "values"? Without the vulnerability of a physical form, "consciousness" might be fundamentally different or impossible.

Biological Problems

The Complexity of Homeostasis

Embodiment highlights another critical truth: the brain survives only because it is sustained by a finely regulated biological environment.

In addition to neural activity and sensory energy, the brain depends on homeostasis—the constant regulation of temperature, pH, energy supply, and metabolic balance (Roh et al., 2016). Even minor changes in these parameters can affect cognitive function, mood, and consciousness (Young et al., 2019). A digital brain will require mechanisms to study not only neurons but also the entire regulatory environment that supports them. Otherwise, we risk creating a static, fragile structure, insufficiently adaptive and resilient to the living brain.

Metabolic Costs of Thinking

The human brain is a real energy center, consuming approximately 20% of the body's total energy, despite accounting for only 2% of its weight. This energy is needed not only for processing but also to maintain the membrane's resting potential. Neurons are like leaky batteries that must be constantly recharged by the sodium-potassium pump (Attwell & Laughlin, 2001).

In the living brain, if energy levels (glucose/ATP) drop, the brain prioritizes certain functions and shuts down others (leading to "brain fog" or loss of consciousness) (López-Gambero et al., 2019). A digital model might also need to simulate this competition for resources. If the digital environment lacks "metabolic stress," AI may never develop the efficiency and "heuristics" (Tversky & Kahneman, 1974) (shortcuts) that define human intuition.

Glymphatic System: The Brain's "Waste Management"

The glymphatic system clears the brain of metabolic waste products (such as beta-amyloid) during sleep. This chemical "reboot" is essential for mental clarity (Iliff et al., 2012). A digital brain that never "sleeps" or "cleanses" itself may suffer from the digital version of toxic information entropy. Preserving personality over time in a simulation may require simulating the periodic degradation and restoration of its own environment.

Vision of Computing Power: Managing Heat and Entropy

Homeostasis refers to the process of self-regulation by which an open system maintains a stable internal environment. Through coordinated responses, the brain ensures a state of dynamic equilibrium; for instance, it triggers sweating during heat exposure to regulate and maintain an optimal body temperature (Tan & Knight, 2018).

Modern supercomputers already experience problems with homeostasis in the form of heat dissipation.

Evolution of Computing

In the future, "brain-scale" computers may use microfluidic cooling where liquid flows through the chips themselves, similar to blood flowing through the brain. This creates a literal physical requirement for "homeostasis" in the hardware.

We often imagine the digital mind as an immortal; however, biological consciousness is a process of constant renewal. Homeostasis teaches us that the self is not a fixed architecture, but a system that must be constantly nourished and maintained in balance. The digital brain may need to experience a "hunger" for data or "fatigue" from processing to truly reflect the adaptive resilience of the human spirit.

Impact on Mental Workload

Taken together, these biological barriers reveal that the brain is much more than just a network of electrical signals. It is a living, chemical, corporeal system, continuously interacting with the body and the environment. To fully replicate the mind, it seems the download must encompass not only its structure and activity, but also the entire biological context that gives rise to thoughts, feelings, and consciousness.

These complexities don't make mind uploading impossible in the future, but they do illustrate why it remains one of the most ambitious scientific projects imaginable. Every layer of biology we overlook—glial function, chemical signaling, hormonal modulation, embodiment—represents a potential gap between a digital copy and a living mind.

Biological barriers remind us that the mind is inseparable from life itself. Neurons, glia, chemistry, and the body form a deeply interdependent system, and consciousness emerges from this interaction.

Philosophical Barriers: Identity Paradoxes—If a Copy is Made, is it "You" or Just a Duplicate?

Even if we were to overcome the technical and biological barriers to mind uploading, a profound philosophical problem remains: what does it mean to be "oneself"? Creating a digital copy of one's consciousness raises profound questions about identity, continuity, and the nature of the self; questions that have puzzled philosophers for centuries, questions we explored in the opening chapters (McAdams et al., 2021).

Continuity of Consciousness

In biology, we experience a "stream of consciousness." Although the atoms in our brain are replaced every few years, the process is continuous. Consciousness uploading, especially "scanning and copying," creates a discontinuity. If a person is scanned while awake and a digital version is turned on, there are now two "persons."

From the perspective of a digital copy, the upload is a success; the consciousness retains the memory of being the original subject only a moment prior. However, from the original individual's perspective, no transition has occurred. They remain seated, unmoved, and unchanged. This discrepancy suggests that information is not synonymous with identity.

Destructive and Non-Destructive Scanning

The loading method changes the philosophical aspects:

- Destructive scanning: This involves slicing the brain at the nanometer level for mapping (as required by modern electron microscopy). Here, the original "individual" ceases to exist. Is this a transference or a death, where a digital heir inherits individual memories?
- Moravec's Transference ("Ship of Theseus"): Hans Moravec proposed a "gradual" upload, in which neurons are replaced one by one with silicon

chips while you're awake (Moravec, 1988). This leads to an identity paradox. At what percentage of silicon do you cease to be a biological human and begin to be a digital simulation? What if the transition is gradual?

The Identity Registry and the Post-Deficient Self

As we consider the capabilities of computers in the near future, the concept of "one body, one mind" may be challenged by distributed identity:

- Future computing systems may move toward blockchain-based identity verification for digital minds. To solve the "duplication problem," a computer system may require a unique "identity key" that can only exist in one place at a time to prevent "forking" of the self.
- The power of multiplicity: Computers of the future will be able to easily run multiple instances of a single neural map. This creates a vision of a future where a single "person" can simultaneously perform a thousand tasks in a virtual cloud, but this leads to a "fragmented self" that may ultimately lose the ability to reintegrate into a unified personality.

Twenty-first-century technological mastery may ultimately face the problem of "identity preservation." If we view the mind as software, we must accept that software can be copied, edited, and deleted. This reduces the self to a collection of data points. While we may in the future achieve "digital immortality" for our thoughts and memories, the actual self, the subjective observer behind your eyes, may be a biological phenomenon that cannot be copied, only simulated.

Teleportation Paradox

These concerns about continuity naturally extend into classic philosophical thought experiments that test our intuitions about survival and duplication.

Does the machine transport an individual, or does it kill an individual and create a new version of the individual somewhere else? Teleportation is like the Ship of Theseus. Our biological brains can already be considered as Ships of Theseus. The atoms in our neurons are constantly being replaced; the molecules that make up your synapses today are different from those you had ten years ago. And yet, we feel like the same person. The difference with mind uploading is that we change the type of "board." We go from carbon-based biological "boards" to silicon-based digital "boards." If the pattern remains the same, does the change in material matter?

For a person in a scanning chair, "uploading" can feel like death. For a person waking up in a cloud, it feels like a miracle. This creates a "survivorship bias" effect in the digital consciousness: every uploaded consciousness will swear the process worked, because those for whom it didn't work (the originals) can no longer complain.

The Theorem on the Impossibility of Cloning

Some researchers have proposed that consciousness may involve quantum processes. Roger Penrose and Stuart Hameroff suggested that microtubules within neurons could host quantum coherence, potentially influencing brain activity at a fundamental level (Hameroff & Penrose, 2014). This is known as the Orchestrated Objective Reduction (Orch-OR) theory. If consciousness indeed depends on quantum states in the brain, then the no-cloning theorem (Wootters & Zurek, 1982) implies that it might be impossible to create a perfect, identical copy of a conscious mind. But it is worth adding that Orch-OR remains highly controversial and is not accepted by mainstream neuroscience.

Thought Experiments and Ethical Implications

Philosopher Derek Parfit has suggested that identity may be less about strict continuity than about relational and functional connections: what matters is not the individual personality, but a network of psychological traits and memories (Parfit, 1984).

However, these distinctions do not resolve ethical and emotional issues. If digital copies experience suffering, who is responsible for it? If they can continue your life, do they inherit your rights and responsibilities? Mind uploading forces us to confront uncomfortable questions about mortality, responsibility, and the nature of existence itself.

Ultimately, the question may not be whether the copy is you, but whether it is conscious and capable of experience. If a digital mind can feel, think, and perceive, it deserves consideration, even if it is not the "original" you. But if consciousness is incommunicable, as some theories suggest, uploading could create a convincing simulation without capturing the living self. Philosophical barriers reveal that mind uploading isn't just a technical or biological problem, but also a profound exploration of what it means to be human (Chalmers, 2010).

Digital Suffering and the Ethics of the "Substrate"

If a digital mind experiences "pain" (a signal of system failure or metabolic stress), is pausing the simulation a moral crime? Engineers often "reset" or "roll back" simulations during testing. However, if the mind is conscious, "reset" is the deletion of a specific timeline of experience. Is "pausing" a digital being a form of imprisonment? Is "deleting" it a form of murder?

Digital Intelligence as a Moral Subject

The principle of substrate neutrality (Bostrom, 2003). This philosophical position asserts that if a system performs the same functions as a biological brain, including the chemical and homeostatic regulations described earlier, then it should have the same moral status. We should distinguish between "simulated pain" (the variable labeled "pain" = 10) and "phenomenal pain" (the actual sensation of pain). If the simulation is so detailed, including hormones such as cortisol and adrenaline, then the digital intelligence is not simply simulating pain; it is embodying it. In the future, a "Digital Bill of Rights" may be needed to protect simulated consciousness from exploitation, endless loops, or forced labor.

These concerns about continuity naturally extend into classic philosophical thought experiments that test our intuitions about survival and duplication.

The "loading" problem is often mistaken for a lack of memory; in reality, it's a lack of "attachment." A mind without a body is a mind without context. To replicate consciousness, we must move away from the metaphor of "computation" and toward the metaphor of "interaction." Future computing must provide a synthetic embodiment, a digital vessel that experiences gravity, friction, and internal "biological" rhythms. Only then will the simulated mind be able to move from "processing data" to "perceiving the world."

References

Atanas, A., et al. (2026). Deep neural networks to register and annotate cells in moving and deforming nervous systems. *eLife*, 15, e108159. doi:10.7554/eLife.108159

Attwell, D., & Laughlin, S. B. (2001). An energy budget for signaling in the grey matter of the brain. *Journal of Cerebral Blood Flow & Metabolism*, 21(10), 1133–1145. doi:10.1097/00004647-200110000-00001

Azevedo, F. A. C., Carvalho, L. R. B., Grinberg, L. T., Farfel, J. M., Ferretti, R. E. L., Leite, R. E. P., Jacob Filho, W., Lent, R., & Herculano-Houzel, S. (2009). Equal numbers of neuronal and nonneuronal cells make the human brain an isometrically scaled-up primate brain. *Journal of Comparative Neurology*, 513(5), 532–541. doi:10.1002/cne.21974

Borroto-Escuela, D. O., Gonzalez-Cristo, E., Ochoa-Torres, V., Serra-Rojas, E. M., Ambrogini, P., Arroyo-García, L. E., & Fuxe, K. (2024). Understanding electrical and chemical transmission in the brain. *Frontiers in Cellular Neuroscience*, 18, Article 1398862. doi:10.3389/fncel.2024.1398862

Bostrom, N. (2003). Are you living in a computer simulation? *Philosophical Quarterly*, 53(211), 243–255.

Chalmers, D. J. (2010). *The character of consciousness*. Oxford University Press.

Damasio, A. R. (2010). *Self comes to mind: Constructing the conscious brain*. Pantheon Books.

Dayan, P., & Huys, Q. J. (2009). Serotonin in affective control. *Annual Review of Neuroscience*, 32, 95–126. doi:10.1146/annurev.neuro.051508.135607

Escalada, P., Ezkurdia, A., Ramírez, M. J., & Solas, M. (2024). Essential role of astrocytes in learning and memory. *International Journal of Molecular Sciences*, 25(3), 1899. doi:10.3390/ijms25031899

Freeman, D., & Odegaard, B. (2025). Transcranial focused ultrasound for identifying the neural substrate of conscious perception. *arXiv preprint*. doi:10.48550/arXiv.2507.08517

Friston, K., Schwartenbeck, P., FitzGerald, T., Moutoussis, M., Behrens, T., & Dolan, R. J. (2013). The anatomy of choice: Active inference and agency. *Frontiers in Human Neuroscience*, 7, Article 598. doi:10.3389/fnhum.2013.00598

Gerstner, W., Kistler, W. M., Naud, R., & Paninski, L. (2014). *Neuronal dynamics: From single neurons to networks and models of cognition.* Cambridge University Press.

Hameroff, S., & Penrose, R. (2014). Consciousness in the universe: A review of the "Orch OR" theory. *Physics of Life Reviews*, 11(1), 39–78. doi:10.1016/j.plrev.2013.08.002

Iliff, J. J., Wang, M., Liao, Y., Plogg, B. A., Peng, W., Gundersen, G. A., Benveniste, H., Vates, G. E., & Nedergaard, M. (2012). A paravascular pathway facilitates CSF flow through the brain parenchyma and the clearance of interstitial solutes, including amyloid β. *Science Translational Medicine*, 4(147), Article 147ra111. doi:10.1126/scitranslmed.3003748

Intel Corporation. (n.d.). Neuromorphic computing: Next generation of AI. https://www.intel.la/content/www/xl/es/research/neuromorphic-computing.htm

Kandel, E. R., Schwartz, J. H., Jessell, T. M., et al. (2012). *Principles of neural science* (5th ed.). McGraw-Hill.

López-Gambero, A. J., Martínez, F., Salazar, K., Vicario, C., & Rodríguez de Fonseca, F. (2019). Brain glucose-sensing mechanism and energy homeostasis. *Molecular Neurobiology*, 56(2), 769–796. doi:10.1007/s12035-018-1099-4

Luca, E., Zitzmann, K., Bornstein, S., Kugelmeier, P., Beuschlein, F., Nölting, S., & Hantel, C. (2023). Three-dimensional models of endocrine organs and target tissues regulated by the endocrine system. *Cancers*, 15(18), 4601. doi:10.3390/cancers15184601

Martins, N. R. B., Erlhagen, W., & Freitas, R. A., Jr. (2012). Non-destructive whole-brain monitoring using nanorobots: Neural electrical data rate requirements. *International Journal of Machine Consciousness*, 4(1), 109–140.

McAdams, D. et al. (2021). Self and identity in personality psychology. *Personality Science*, 2.

Mehrabi, A., Sreenivasan, N., Gunawardana, U., & Gargiulo, G. (2026). Hybrid spike-encoded spiking neural networks for real-time EEG seizure detection: A comparative benchmark. *Biomimetics*, 11(1), 75. doi:10.3390/biomimetics11010075

Moiz, S. A., Alshaikh, M. S., & Alahmadi, A. N. M. (2025). Organic bioelectronics: Diversity of electronics along with biosciences. *Biosensors*, 15(9), 587. doi:10.3390/bios15090587

Moravec, H. P. (1988). *Mind children: The future of robot and human intelligence.* Harvard University Press.

Neuroscience News. (2025, November 17). Supercomputer enables first-ever biophysically accurate whole-brain simulation. https://neurosciencenews.com/supercomputer-cortex-mapping-29938/

Parfit, D. (1984). *Reasons and persons.* Oxford University Press.

Petersson, M., & Uvnäs-Moberg, K. (2024). Interactions of oxytocin and dopamine—Effects on behavior in health and disease. *Biomedicines*, 12(11), 2440. doi:10.3390/biomedicines12112440

Pezzulo, G., Parr, T., Cisek, P., Clark, A., & Friston, K. (2024). Generating meaning: Active inference and the scope and limits of passive AI. *Trends in Cognitive Sciences*, 28(2), 97–112. doi:10.1016/j.tics.2023.10.002

Roh, E., Song, D., & Kim, M. S. (2016). Emerging role of the brain in the homeostatic regulation of energy and glucose metabolism. *Experimental & Molecular Medicine*, 48 (3), Article e216. doi:10.1038/emm.2016.4

Service, R. F. (2024). Microchips that mimic the human brain could make AI far more energy-efficient. *Science.* https://www.science.org/content/article/microchips-mimic-human-brain-could-make-ai-far-more-energy-efficient

Tan, C. L., & Knight, Z. A. (2018). Regulation of body temperature by the nervous system. *Neuron*, 98(1), 31–48. doi:10.1016/j.neuron.2018.02.022

Teleanu, R. I., Niculescu, A.-G., Roza, E., Vladâcenco, O., Grumezescu, A. M., & Teleanu, D. M. (2022). Neurotransmitters—Key factors in neurological and neurodegenerative disorders of the central nervous system. *International Journal of Molecular Sciences*, 23(11), 5954. doi:10.3390/ijms23115954

Tian, X., Bai, J., Liu, D., & authors. (2025). A fully-integrated flexible in-sensor computing circuit based on gel-gated organic electrochemical transistors. *npj Flexible Electronics*, 9(1), Article 90. doi:10.1038/s41528-025-00472-x

Tversky, A., & Kahneman, D. (1974). Judgment under uncertainty: Heuristics and biases. *Science*, 185(4157), 1124–1131. doi:10.1126/science.185.4157.1124

Vallverdú, J., & Rius, G. (2025). NeuroQ: Quantum-inspired brain emulation. *Biomimetics*, 10, 516. doi:10.3390/biomimetics10080516

Wootters, W. K., & Zurek, W. H. (1982). A single quantum cannot be cloned. *Nature*, 299(5886), 802–803.

Young, H. A., Cousins, A., Johnston, S., Fletcher, I., & Benton, D. (2019). Autonomic adaptations mediate the effect of hydration on brain functioning and mood: Evidence from two randomized controlled trials. *Scientific Reports*, 9(1), Article 16412. doi:10.1038/s41598-019-52775-5

Zhang, Z., et al. (2025). High-speed neural imaging with multiplexed miniaturized two-photon microscopy. *Cell Reports Methods*, 5(12), 101221. doi:10.1016/j.crmeth.2025.101221

6 Experiments on the Edge of Science

Introduction

Chapter 5 revealed the immense technical, biological, and philosophical barriers to mind uploading. The challenge is not merely computational, it is structural, chemical, embodied, and deeply tied to identity itself. If the brain is a dynamic, living process rather than a static circuit, then replicating it appears almost impossibly complex. And yet, despite these obstacles, science has not stood still.

Across neuroscience laboratories, AI research centers, and emerging neurotechnology startups, experiments are already probing the boundaries between biology and computation. Partial simulations, neural interfaces, brain–machine integrations, and digital reconstructions of small neural systems are beginning to test the limits of what can be captured, modeled, and reproduced. This chapter turns from theory to practical achievements.

The Connectome

A connectome is a comprehensive structural or functional map of the neural connections in the brain. The word "connectome" didn't exist until 2005. It was independently and almost simultaneously coined by two researchers: Olaf Sporns, a neurobiologist at Indiana University, and Patrick Hagmann, a Swiss physician and engineer completing his doctorate in Lausanne. Sporns, working with Giulio Tononi and Rolf Koetter, published a paper in September 2005, titled "The Human Connectome: A Structural Description of the Human Brain," in which he proposed that neuroscience needed a systematic effort to map the complete structural connectivity of the human brain and that this effort needed a name (Sporns et al., 2005).

Hagmann used the word in his dissertation, submitted that same year, unaware of Sporns's article (Hagmann, 2005). The fact that two researchers from different countries arrived at the same term at the same time was no coincidence. It was a sign that the concept had been developing for decades, and the field of research was ripe for it.

DOI: 10.4324/9781003794677-7

Sebastian Seung has made a significant contribution to popularizing the connectome as a term among the public. In 2010, Seung gave a TED talk viewed by millions and made a statement that was both scientifically and philosophically compelling: "I am my connectome" (Seung, 2010). Seung argued that "I" am not the neurons themselves (neurons die and are replaced throughout life), but the structure of connections between them. It is in this structure that memory, personality, and the record of one's life are stored. If the connectome could be fully mapped and preserved, then in some meaningful sense, a person could be preserved along with it. His 2012 book, also titled "The Connectome" (Seung, 2013), brought these ideas to a wider audience and even sparked a public debate about the possibility of mind uploading, previously confined to science fiction and philosophy seminars.

In 2012, Seung founded the EyeWire project (https://eyewire.org/explore), an online game that engaged people in tracking neurons in the mouse retina, a collaborative connectomics project. As of 2025, EyeWire had been played by approximately 350,000 people and had resulted in 6,000 neurons being tracked (Sterling, 2025).

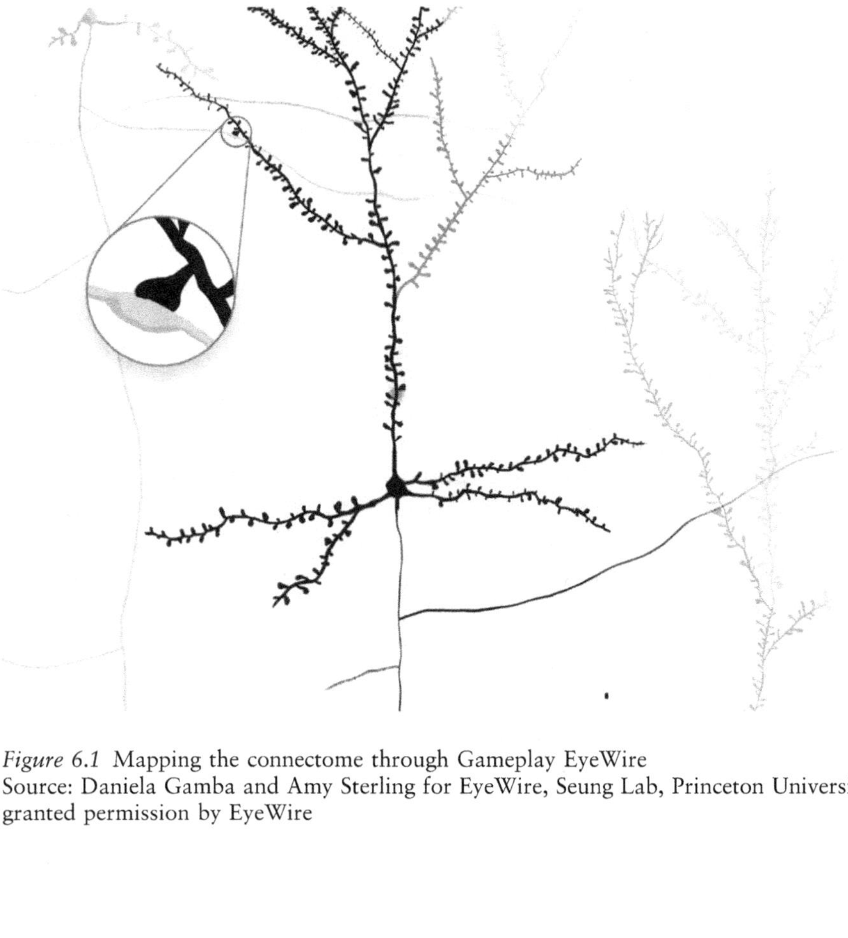

Figure 6.1 Mapping the connectome through Gameplay EyeWire
Source: Daniela Gamba and Amy Sterling for EyeWire, Seung Lab, Princeton University, granted permission by EyeWire

Players competed to construct three-dimensional neural structures by coloring volumes in stacks of images, guided by algorithms that processed the bulk of the tracing but still required human judgment to resolve ambiguous boundaries. EyeWire demonstrated that the sheer scale of connectomics data, the reason why manually mapping the human brain takes geological timescales, could ultimately be addressed not only by more sophisticated algorithms but also by the distributed intelligence of thousands of human minds.

This chapter first traces the practical path to connectome implementation and examines three of the most popular projects, starting with a worm with a cluster of 302 neurons, then a fruit fly with a brain composed of 100,000 neurons, and finally, work on a single human brain. The logical starting point for experimentation is obvious: before we can model the mind, we must first map it.

The Caenorhabditis elegans Connectome: The First Map of a Nervous System

The story begins with a worm barely visible to the naked eye and a group of scientists who believed that understanding life itself could begin by mapping every single connection within it. The organism was Caenorhabditis elegans, a soil nematode about 1 millimeter long, composed of exactly 959 somatic cells in adult hermaphrodites, of which exactly 302 are neurons. It was precisely this simplicity that made it irresistible to researchers in the early 1960s, long before the term "connectome" was coined.

This was a nervous system small enough to be fully mapped, but complex enough to reproduce real-world behavior: feeding, mating, fleeing danger, seeking warmth.

The project's visionary was Sydney Brenner, a South African-born molecular biologist working at the Medical Research Council's Laboratory of Molecular Biology in Cambridge, England. Brenner had already helped decipher the genetic code and was looking for his next big challenge. In 1963, he wrote a now-famous letter proposing C. elegans as an ideal model organism for studying how genes control the development and function of the nervous system (Brenner, 1963). He was convinced that the key to understanding the brain lay in a complete understanding of a simpler system, one in which every cell could

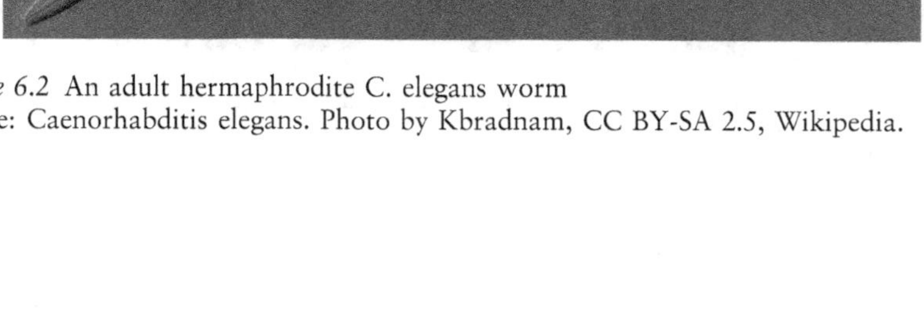

Figure 6.2 An adult hermaphrodite C. elegans worm
Source: Caenorhabditis elegans. Photo by Kbradnam, CC BY-SA 2.5, Wikipedia.

be identified, named, and tracked in individual animals. The project's goal was not simply to observe the worm but to decipher it to map the connections of a living nervous system.

Brenner's instinct proved far-sighted, but its implementation required decades of painstaking, almost monastic, work. This task fell largely to John White, Eileen Southgate, Nichol Thomson, and Sydney Brenner himself, working throughout the 1970s and early 1980s at the MRC laboratory in Cambridge. Their method was electron microscopy, the only technology at the time capable of resolving the finest fibers and nanoscale connections of individual nerve cells.

The scale of the work accomplished is difficult to fully appreciate today. Over the course of approximately 15 years, the team generated and analyzed over 20,000 electron micrographs. Each neuron had to be tracked across hundreds of individual sections, like assembling a three-dimensional puzzle from thousands of nearly identical pieces. Errors were costly: a single misidentified synapse could distort the map of the entire neural circuit. The researchers developed complex color-coding systems and hand-drawn diagrams to track which neurons belonged to which. Computers weren't powerful enough to assist with the actual tracking; it all relied on human vision, human memory, and human patience.

In 1986, the landmark paper "The Structure of the Nervous System of the Nematode Caenorhabditis elegans" by White, Southgate, Thomson, and Brenner (White et al., 1986) was published in the Philosophical Transactions of the

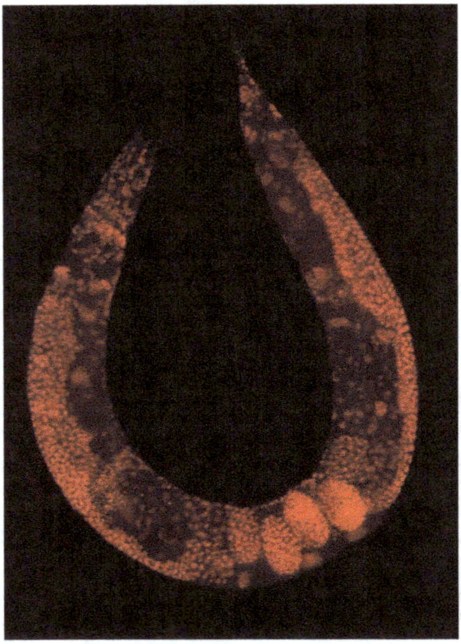

Figure 6.3 C. elegans with the fluorescent dye to highlight the nuclei of all cells
Source: Quadell, CC BY 2.5, 2005, Wikipedia.

Royal Society of London. It described 302 neurons, approximately 7,000 synaptic connections, and 2,000 neuromuscular junctions. The connectome, a term not yet coined but already an established concept, was complete. It was one of the most detailed biological reconstructions ever produced, and it earned Sydney Brenner, John Sulston, and Robert Horvitz the Nobel Prize in Physiology or Medicine in 2002, recognizing the fundamental importance of their research on C. elegans for understanding organ development and programmed cell death (The Nobel Assembly at the Karolinska Institutet, 2002).

However, the limitations of this achievement soon began to become apparent. The connectome was a map; a diagram showing which neurons were physically connected to which. But a diagram is not the same as understanding how this logic works. The connectome could not tell researchers about the strength of individual synapses, how this strength changed over time, or how neuromodulatory substances such as dopamine and serotonin altered the behavior of entire neural circuits in response to the worm's internal state or the external environment.

This became especially problematic when researchers attempted to use the connectome to create computational models of C. elegans behavior. If the connectome truly encoded the worm's behavioral repertoire, then a sufficiently accurate simulation of its 302 neurons and their connections should reproduce the animal's movements and reactions. Early models proved disappointing. The worm's simple sinusoidal crawling pattern, its withdrawal reflex in response to touch, its chemotaxis to food behaviors that any living specimen performed effortlessly proved incredibly difficult to reproduce in simulation. The models moved irregularly, or didn't move at all, or moved in ways that made them unrecognizable as wormlike.

The open-source OpenWorm project (https://openworm.org/), launched in 2011 by a team of researchers and software engineers, was the most recent attempt to model the complete nervous system of C. elegans in software (Szigeti et al., 2014). By combining connectome data from 1986 with more recent electrophysiological measurements, the project aimed to create a digital worm capable of exhibiting a full range of natural behaviors. This was inspiring work, and it made some progress.

In 2014, one team even loaded a simulation of the C. elegans connectome into a small wheeled robot, claiming that the robot navigated its environment using the worm's own neural logic (MacDonald, 2017).

But the more closely researchers examined the problem, the more its shortcomings became apparent. Machine learning algorithms trained to identify active neurons in C. elegans imaging data achieved an accuracy of approximately 78%; a strong result, but it left nearly one in four neurons unidentified or misidentified in any given sample (Yu et al., 2021).

Some neurons appeared only in a minority of individuals, varying in number and location from one worm to another, undermining the assumption that a single canonical connectome could represent all members of a species. The dynamic properties of synapses—how their strength was modulated by experience, hunger, temperature, or developmental stage—remained entirely outside

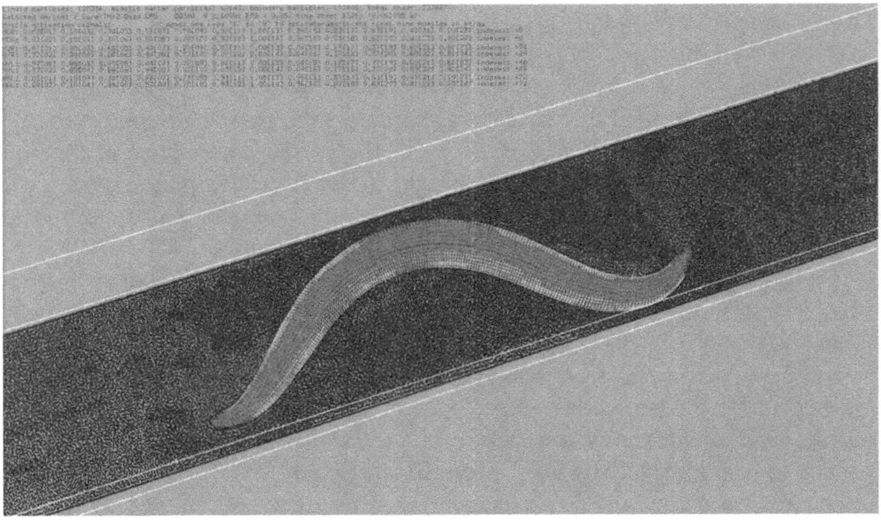

Figure 6.4 Simulated body of the worm on OpenWorm software
Source: Image courtesy of OpenWorm Project (https://openworm.org).

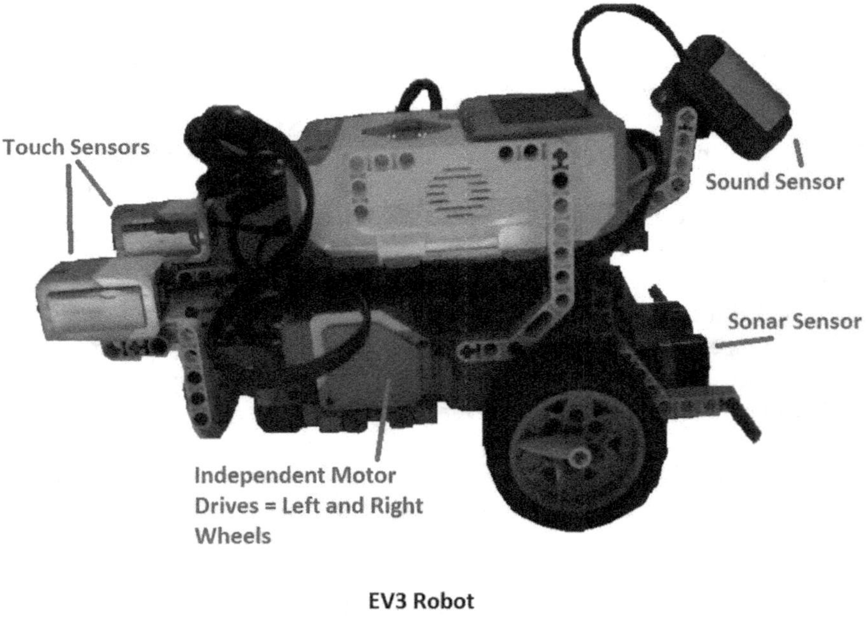

Figure 6.5 Robot navigating using a worm's neural connectome
Source: Image courtesy of the Connectome Engine Project (http://www.connectomeengine.com).

the purview of the connectome. A map compiled at a single point in time based on a single, fixed pattern could not capture the constant flux of a living system.

Thus, the C. elegans connectome demonstrated that it is possible to map the complete pathways of the nervous system, essentially creating a new field of science. And it equally clearly demonstrated that a single pathway map is insufficient to explain or reproduce the behavior of even the simplest known nervous system.

Drosophila Melanogaster: Scaling Up the Challenge

If C. elegans showed scientists what a complete connectome could and couldn't tell them, the next logical step was to apply the same approach on a larger scale and using far more sophisticated tools. The organism chosen for this next step was Drosophila melanogaster, the common fruit fly.

With approximately 100,000 neurons, its brain is more than 330 times larger than that of C. elegans, yet orders of magnitude simpler than that of a mouse or a human (Kasture et al., 2018).

Fruit flies have been one of the most productive subjects of biological research for over a century ever since Thomas Hunt Morgan first used them to map genes onto chromosomes at Columbia University in the early 1900s (National Human Genome Research Institute, n.d.). They reproduce within two weeks, tolerate genetic manipulation extremely well, and their nervous system supports a rich repertoire of behaviors: navigation, courtship, aggression, learning, and memory.

The most significant attempt to map the fly brain was undertaken at the Janelia Research Campus, a division of the Howard Hughes Institute for Medical Research, opened in 2006 in Ashburn, Virginia (Rubin, 2006). Janelia (https://www.janelia.org/) was originally conceived as an unusual facility, a place where scientists could pursue long, expensive, and risky projects that would otherwise struggle to secure grant funding. Mapping the entire connectome of a fly brain fit this description perfectly. The project, which ultimately took 12 years and cost approximately 40 million dollars, was led by a rotating group of neuroscientists, electron microscopy specialists, and computer scientists. Key

Figure 6.6 Drosophila melanogaster feeding on a banana
Source: Sanjay Acharya, CC BY-SA 4.0, 2017, Wikipedia.

figures included Davi Bock, who developed much of the high-throughput imaging strategy, and the teams responsible for what became known as the "half-brain" project—the reconstruction of approximately half a fly brain, focusing on the areas most important for memory, learning, and navigation. The researchers believed that understanding how flies form and retrieve memories at the level of individual synapses could reveal universal computational principles applicable to brains of all sizes, including our own (Schlegel et al., 2024).

The technical complexity of the project dwarfed all previous efforts with C. elegans. While the entire nervous system of a worm was mapped using thousands of electron micrographs, a single cubic millimeter of fly brain tissue generates petabytes of raw image data. The fly brain had to be chemically preserved, embedded in resin, and cut into sections approximately 20 nanometers thick, much thinner than the sections used in worm research in the 1970s, requiring a new generation of automated slicing devices to produce them reliably. Each section was then examined using a focused ion beam (FIB) scanning electron microscope technology that didn't exist when the C. elegans project began. The resulting image stacks were so voluminous that no human team could have manually tracked the neurons in a reasonable timeframe.

Janelia collaborated with Google to develop the computing infrastructure needed to process the reconstruction. The Google team developed a suite of deep learning algorithms specifically, convolutional neural networks trained to segment individual cells across sequential image slices, recognize membranes between neurons, and trace axons and dendrites in three-dimensional space (Xu et al., 2020). The software, eventually released as part of the VAST and Neuroglancer platforms, allowed researchers to navigate the reconstructed brain as if they were flying through a three-dimensional landscape of neurons.

But the algorithms were imperfect. Ultimately, the project employed a dedicated team of proofreaders who spent years reviewing algorithmic solutions, correcting errors, and inspecting synaptic connections one by one. The resulting data set, covering approximately 25,000 neurons and 20 million synaptic connections in just one hemisphere of the brain, weighed in at around 100 terabytes of raw data, which was compressed to a more manageable, but still massive, 100 gigabytes for Scheffer's published reconstruction (Scheffer et al., 2020).

When a study on the hemibrain connectome was published in eLife in 2020, it provided an unprecedented glimpse into brain organization (Scheffer et al., 2020). For the first time, researchers were able to visualize the complete structure of the mushroom bodies, the primary memory structures of the fly, and trace the precise circuits through which sensory experience was encoded, stored, and retrieved. They discovered that memory circuits are far more recurrent and feedback-intensive than anyone had expected, based solely on physiological experiments. They identified previously unknown neuron types, mapped the precise architecture of the central complex responsible for navigation and spatial orientation, and discovered organizational motifs repeating patterns of connectivity that emerged independently across multiple brain regions, hinting at deep computational principles that evolution had discovered and reused.

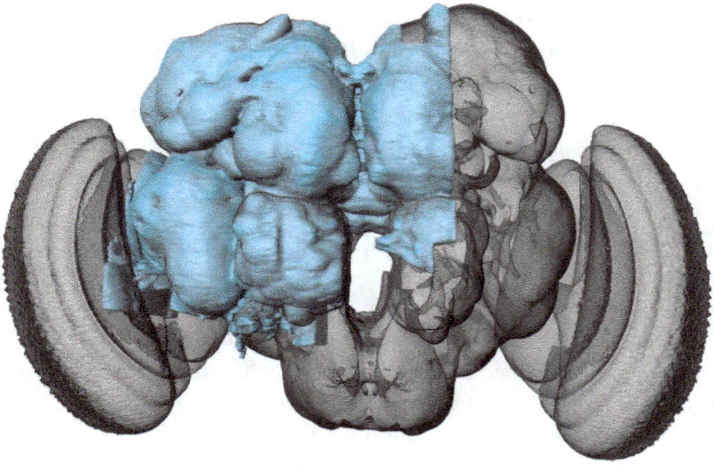

Figure 6.7 The hemibrain and some basic statistics
Note: The highlighted area shows the portion of the central brain that was visualized and reconstructed, superimposed on a grayscale image of the entire Drosophila brain.
Source: Scheffer et al. (2020), A connectome and analysis of the adult Drosophila central brain, eLife, 9, CC BY.

However, even this result only told part of the story. The Hemibrane project mapped one hemisphere of the fly brain, not the entire central nervous system, not both sexes, and not the ventral neural canal, the region that controls body muscles and integrates sensory signals from the wings, legs, and abdomen. Completion of the map came later.

In October 2024, an international team of researchers published the complete connectome of the entire central nervous system of a male fruit fly; the brain and ventral nerve canal combined including 166,000 neurons, tens of millions of synaptic connections, and the classification of 11,691 different cell types. Every connection was verified, annotated, and labeled. Neurons specific to each sex were identified and cataloged. The male CNS connectome became the most comprehensive neural map of any organism with a complex brain ever created, and it was not the result of 15 years of manual work by a small team from Cambridge, but in much less time, thanks to the machine learning infrastructure that the Janelia–Google collaboration helped create.

Comparative Analysis of the Male and Female Drosophila Connectomes

Perhaps the most scientifically striking result of obtaining the complete male connectome was that it allowed comparison with previously mapped female brains. For the first time in biology, researchers were able to examine structural differences between the male and female nervous systems, not as statistical population averages, but as precise, circuit-by-circuit comparisons. The differences were both expected and unexpected. As predicted, the circuits governing reproductive behavior differed significantly. Specific neurons present in males but absent in females, and vice versa, explained long-observed differences in courtship, aggression, and mating behavior in ways that purely physiological or genetic studies could only speculate about. But the comparisons also revealed that many circuits thought to be identical in both sexes exhibited subtle differences in structure, the functional significance of which remains entirely unknown. The connectome opened up a new set of questions: not only what is connected, but also why certain connections differ and what these differences mean for an animal's life experience (Berg et al., 2025).

Yet technological progress is evident; studying 302 neurons took 15 years and the entire careers of a generation of scientists, while now, thanks to automated imaging, deep learning, a team of comparable size needs several years to study 166,000 neurons. Yet the fundamental limitation identified in the C. elegans work has not been overcome, it has simply been magnified. The fly connectome is a structural map. It does not record the states of neuronal activity, the concentrations of neuromodulatory substances acting on different brain regions at different points in time, or how synaptic weights change as the fly learns from experience. A fly that has recently starved navigates its environment completely differently than a well-fed fly, even though the connections between them are identical. The map does not reflect hunger, fear, fatigue, or the subtle history of a life lived. These are not the failures of the connectome project, they are the questions it raises.

Allen's Map

The fruit fly gave us the first glimpse of how memory and navigation are organized at the level of individual synapses. The achievements were significant and both were ultimately made possible by the very small size of the organisms studied. When scaled up to the human brain, with its 86 billion neurons and approximately 100 trillion synaptic connections, all the methods that worked so elegantly with the fruit fly become difficult to implement. The human brain weighs approximately 1,400 grams. The nervous system of C. elegans, by comparison, weighs less than a milligram. Mapping the brain at the resolution necessary to observe individual synapses, with the imaging speeds available even today, would take many, many years. This is a challenge that cannot be solved by patience or funding alone. This requires a completely different strategy, and before any strategy for replicating or simulating the human brain can succeed, the most basic condition must be met: the creation of an accurate, comprehensive, and highly accurate map of what the human brain actually looks like.

For most of the twentieth century, such a map did not exist, at least not in a form that would satisfy neuroscientists asking serious questions. The brain atlases that doctors and researchers relied on largely originated with the work of Korbinian Brodmann, a German neurologist who in 1909 published his landmark classification of the human cerebral cortex into 52 distinct regions based on cellular architecture visible under a light microscope (Zilles & Amunts, 2010).

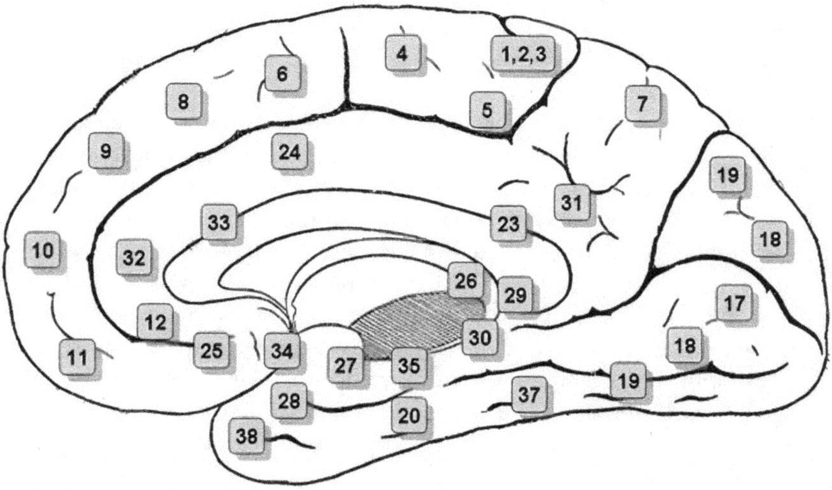

Figure 6.8 The Brodmann areas of a human brain
Source: Wikipedia Commons, Public Domain.

Brodmann's map was a remarkable achievement for its time and remains influential today. However, it was compiled manually from a single brain at low resolution, using staining methods that revealed relatively little about the molecular identity or connectivity of the observed cells. For over a century, medicine continued to refer to atlases that were essentially variations on this same limited basis.

Interestingly, the man who decided to change this wasn't a neuroscientist. It was Paul Allen, the co-founder of Microsoft, who made his fortune building the software infrastructure of the modern world and who, in the last decades of his life, turned his attention and resources to problems he believed were important. Allen had a personal interest in neuroscience, and in 2003, he donated $100 million to establish the Allen Institute for Brain Research in Seattle, Washington (https://alleninstitute.org/), an institution modeled after the large-scale, problem-oriented research model he had observed succeeding in the tech industry (Allen Institute, 2003). By the time of his death in 2018 from non-Hodgkin's lymphoma, Allen had invested over $500 million of his personal fortune into the Institute and its associated projects (Herper, 2012, para. 4). He did not live to see the full fruits of these investments, but the institution he founded continued his work.

The Institute's first major product was the Allen Mouse Brain Atlas, completed in 2006, which mapped gene expression across the entire mouse brain at cellular resolution. It was the first atlas to cover the entire mammalian brain, with detailed descriptions of every gene, and it immediately became one of the most frequently used resources in neuroscience (Goyal et al., 2020). But a mouse was still not a human.

Transferring data from mice to humans required a new project and a new sample. Allen's human brain atlas, published in 2013, was created using a single donor brain, that of a 34-year-old woman with no known neurological or psychiatric history (Ding et al., 2016).

The choice of a young, neurologically healthy donor was deliberate: the researchers wanted to obtain a reference atlas reflecting the typical adult brain, free from the structural changes associated with aging, disease, or injury. The brain was processed using a combination of techniques that collectively represented cutting-edge advances in neuroanatomical technology. Before sectioning the intact brain, high-resolution magnetic resonance imaging and diffusion-weighted imaging were performed, creating a three-dimensional reference volume within which each subsequent measurement could be precisely localized. The brain was then physically dissected into 1,356 large sections, each of which was examined at a cellular resolution of 1 micrometer per pixel, high enough to distinguish individual cell bodies using immunohistochemistry and Nissl staining, techniques that reveal both cell shape and the molecular markers that distinguish different cell types.

To obtain images of this resolution across the entire hemisphere of the human brain, the Institute had to develop new equipment. A scanner capable of capturing images of entire brain sections with micrometer resolution equipment was designed and built specifically for this project.

The resulting atlas contains fully annotated images of 862 distinct brain structures, including 117 white matter fibers, as well as previously uncharacterized structures revealed by cytoarchitectural and chemoarchitectural analysis, the study of cell arrangement and molecular markers that standard staining was previously too crude to detect. Crucially, all microscopic annotations were superimposed on intact reference MRI images, creating a bridge between the macroscopic anatomy visible in brain imaging and the microscopic cellular organization visible only under a microscope. For the first time, researchers could point to a region on MRI and know precisely what cell types were located there, how they were arranged, and what molecular markers they expressed (Ding et al., 2016).

Human Connectome Project

Around the same time, the Human Connectome Project (HCP) (https://www.humanconnectome.org/), a large NIH-funded initiative launched in 2009, was creating its own human brain atlas using high-resolution MRI scans of 210 healthy adults. The HCP atlas captured population-wide patterns of brain organization with impressive statistical power, and its cortical segmentation, published in 2016, identified 360 distinct cortical regions, nearly double the number of regions in Brodmann's original map. But MRI, no matter how sophisticated, cannot distinguish individual neurons or synapses. It operates at a millimeter scale; Allen's atlas operated at a micrometer scale, a difference in resolution of three orders of magnitude. These two projects complemented rather than competed: the HCP offered breadth of coverage and statistical generalizability, while the Allen's atlas offered cellular depth and molecular precision. Most importantly, the Allen Institute made its atlas freely available online, integrating it with existing gene expression databases, so any researcher anywhere in the world could discover which genes are active in a given brain structure by correlating this information with cellular anatomy and location in the living brain, as determined by MRI (Glasser et al., 2016).

To answer the central question of this book—whether it will ever be possible to copy, download, or accurately simulate the human brain—the Allen atlas represents something essential, easily underestimated. A connectome, whether that of a worm or a fly, is a map of connections. But before map connections can occur, we need to know what exactly to connect: what cell types exist, where they live, how they're organized, and what molecular identity distinguishes one from another. The Allen atlas provides just that. It's the foundational layer without which no serious human connectome project can begin. When researchers at the Allen Institute or elsewhere talk about eventually mapping the human connectome, they're not starting from scratch, they're

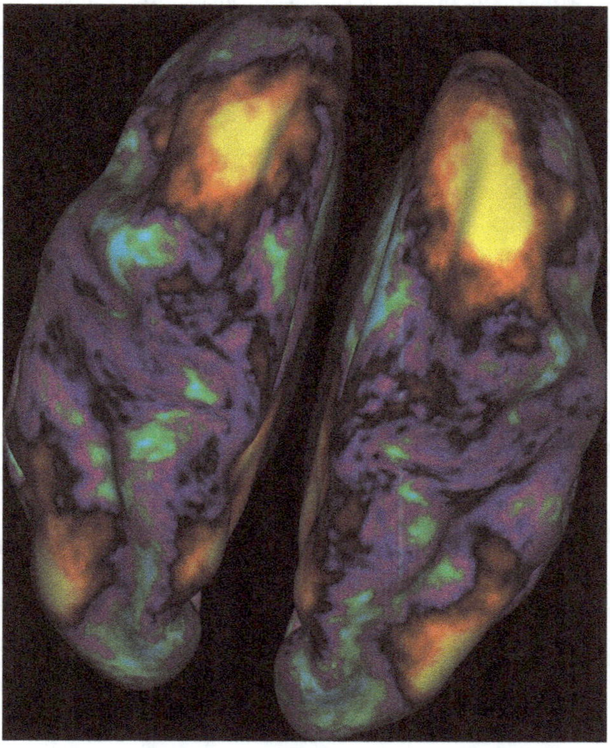

Figure 6.9 Resting-state functional connectivity map of the human cerebral cortex
Source: Image courtesy of M. F. Glasser and S. M. Smith for the WU-Minn HCP Consortium, Human Connectome Project (http://humanconnectome.org).

building on the increasingly detailed picture of the brain's cellular geography, assembled section by section and gene by gene over the past two decades. The worm showed us that a map is possible. The fly showed us how quickly tools can improve. Allen's atlas showed us what the final result actually looks like, at a resolution no one had ever seen before.

Now that researchers can see with cellular precision the structures that comprise the human brain and how they are organized, they can begin to ask which neural networks are responsible for memory, perception, and decision-making; how different areas interact to create a unified conscious experience; and what structural patterns distinguish conscious from unconscious information processing. The atlas alone can't answer these questions. But without it, they cannot be meaningfully asked. Every subsequent ambitious project, every attempt to model a neural circuit, upload a mind, or reconstruct the basis of thought, builds on the foundation laid by Allen's investment and the Institute's work (Ding et al., 2016).

Connectomics Lessons

Connectome projects highlight both the promise and limitations of modern neuroscience. They demonstrate that brain mapping is fundamentally possible, but they also show that structure alone may not be sufficient to describe cognitive processes or consciousness. The brain is a dynamic, adaptive system, not simply a static network.

Nevertheless, these experiments provide invaluable information. They help uncover fundamental principles of neural organization, test computational models, and lay the foundation for future brain simulations. Even partial maps of mammalian neural circuits can aid in the development of artificial intelligence (AI), neuroprosthetics, and our understanding of disease.

Beyond the Dominant Path: Other Roads Toward the Brain's Map

Electron microscopy is a slow and labor-intensive method at scale. And, as we have seen, even mapping a portion of a fruit fly's brain required a multi-year project costing tens of millions of dollars. This is why other lines of research are developing in parallel, some are attempting to solve the imaging problem from a completely different physical perspective, while others are approaching the brain's architecture not through its pathways but through its chemistry, development, or hardware analogs. None of these alternative approaches has yet produced a complete connectome, and none has yet displaced electron microscopy as the primary tool in this field. However, several have made noteworthy progress.

X-Ray Nanotomograph

One of the most promising recent alternatives to electron microscopy is X-ray nanotomography, a method that uses focused high-energy X-rays instead of electrons to image tissue at nanoscale resolution. The theoretical appeal of this method is enormous: unlike electrons, X-rays can penetrate much larger volumes of tissue without the need for physical dissection. If this method worked at sufficient resolution, it would allow researchers to obtain three-dimensional images of an intact tissue sample and reconstruct its structure computationally without cutting it, thereby preserving the sample and, in principle, significantly speeding up the imaging process (Humbel et al., 2024).

Until recently, the problem was that the intense X-rays required to achieve nanoresolution were also powerful enough to destroy the tissue being imaged. The sample degraded and disintegrated before a full data set could be obtained (Holler et al., 2017).

However, in December 2025, a team of researchers led by Carles Bosch and Andreas Schäfer of the Francis Crick Institute in London, working with colleagues from the Paul Scherrer Institute in Switzerland and the European Synchrotron Radiation Facility in France, published a paper demonstrating the feasibility of overcoming this barrier. Their solution was elegant, thanks to a combination of components: they developed a cryogenic platform to stabilize the tissue during irradiation, implemented non-rigid tomographic reconstruction algorithms capable of compensating for minor sample deformation, and most importantly embedded the tissue in a special epoxy resin, originally developed for the nuclear and aerospace industries, which proved far more radiation-resistant than conventional biological sample preparation materials. Tissue samples embedded in this resin withstood X-ray doses exceeding 10 billion grays, far above the threshold that would destroy biological samples prepared using conventional methods. The resulting images, with an isotropic resolution of less than 40 nanometers, were sufficient to identify individual bundles of axons, dendrites, and synapses in mouse brain tissue without physical dissection (Bosch et al., 2025).

Figure 6.10 Volumetric imaging with isotropic resolution allows for exploration of the brain along any virtual slicing direction

Source: Reproduced from Humbel et al. (2024),

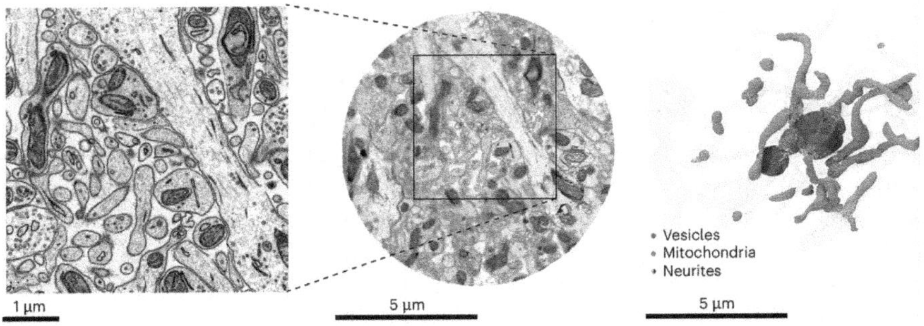

Figure 6.11 A magnified X-ray image of mouse brain tissue showing minute structures such as individual cells and the space around them, obtained using an extremely small microscope without cutting the brain

Source: Reproduced from Bosch et al. (2025), Nature Methods, 2025, CC BY 4.0.

When the team compared their X-ray results with an existing reference method—focused ion beam scanning electron microscopy of the same tissue—they found that more than two-thirds of the synapses identified in the electron microscope images were also recognized in the X-ray images.

This approach is not yet a replacement for electron microscopy. The resolution remains somewhat lower, and imaging speed still needs to improve before millimeter-scale brain imaging is feasible. But this approach points to a future where large volumes of tissue can be imaged non-destructively, much faster than serial sectioning, using X-ray beamlines already available at synchrotron facilities worldwide and freely accessible to researchers. Fourth-generation synchrotron radiation sources, which deliver significantly higher X-ray brightness than older facilities, could further increase throughput by orders of magnitude. For the purpose of mapping the human brain, or any brain larger than a fly's, speed and non-destructive imaging are not just technical conveniences.

Map of Neuron Origin

A second, very different line of progress emerged at the end of 2025, when several papers were published simultaneously in *Nature*, presenting the first comprehensive atlas of mammalian brain development, a map not of how neurons are connected in the adult brain, but of how neurons arise in the first place (Gao et al., 2025; Keefe et al., 2025; Corrigan et al., 2025). Using single-cell and spatial transcriptomics techniques that allow the gene expression profile of individual cells to be read while preserving their location within the tissue, research teams tracked hundreds of thousands of early brain cells in both the human and mouse cerebral cortex, capturing with high precision the molecular events that transform embryonic stem cells into the diverse population of neurons and accessory cells that make up the mature brain. The atlas maps the step-by-step developmental pathway of cellular differentiation: which genes are turned on and off at each stage, which cell types emerge in what order, and how the spatial architecture of the developing cerebral cortex is formed.

Every connectomics project described so far begins with the adult brain; it maps the structure of something already built. But if we ever hope to truly understand, model, or replicate the human brain, we need to understand not only its architecture in adulthood but also how that architecture emerges from the developmental instructions encoded in its biology.

Artificial Neurons

The third line of progress moves in a completely different direction from mapping the brain to creating something that works like it. In October 2025, a team led by Professor Joshua Yang of the University of Southern California's Viterbi School of Engineering published a paper in the journal *Nature Electronics* describing artificial neurons that not only mathematically mimic biological neural behavior, as traditional software-based neural networks do, but also physically reproduce the underlying electrochemical processes (Zhao et al., 2025). The key innovation is a device called a diffusion memristor, a component in which silver ions move through an oxide material in response to electrical signals, generating pulses that precisely mimic how calcium and sodium ions in biological neurons generate action potentials.

The resulting artificial neuron requires only three components, one memristor, one resistor, and one transistor, occupying the space of a single transistor on a chip, compared to the tens or hundreds of transistors required in traditional neuromorphic designs. Power consumption is reduced by orders of magnitude compared to existing approaches.

It's important to clearly define what this achievement is and what it isn't. A diffusion memristor is not a neuron. It mimics certain aspects of a neuron's electrical behavior using a physically similar but chemically distinct process. The team acknowledges that silver ions, the mechanism used in their device, are incompatible with standard semiconductor manufacturing, meaning the path to large-scale integration is still unclear. Of course, this is still early research, and the gap between demonstrating a single artificial neuron on a chip in a university cleanroom and creating a functional neuromorphic system at the scale of the brain is enormous. If we succeed in creating artificial neurons that physically embody the dynamics of biological computation not simulated in software running on von Neumann hardware, but implemented in the physics of materials, then the long-term prospect of creating a hardware analog of the brain will at least become feasible.

Three different projects, published in late 2025 (Gao et al., 2025; Keefe et al., 2025; Corrigan et al., 2025), each approach the brain from a different perspective: visualizing it without destroying it, mapping its development from the very beginning, creating hardware that functions as it does. None of them answers the question this book asks. None of them, taken individually, brings us significantly closer to replicating the human mind. But together, they illustrate something important about the state of the field: the dominant approach connectomics using electron microscopy has serious limitations, and serious scientists are working on alternatives.

Simulating the Brain: From Single Neurons to Whole-Brain Models

Everything described in this chapter so far falls under one category of task: mapping. The goal is to observe the brain as it is to record its structure, cell types, connections, and developmental history with ever-increasing precision and completeness. But mapping is not the same as understanding. Moving from a map to such understanding requires modelling, creating a working computational model that can be run, tested, manipulated, and observed in ways that a fixed anatomical image never could. Neuroscience has been developing modeling tools in parallel with mapping tools for decades, and these tools have become truly powerful. Moreover, for the question this book asks, they are perhaps the most directly relevant technology of all. Mapping shows us what the brain contains. Modeling is the first attempt to make it work.

First Steps Towards Brain Simulation: NEURON

The oldest and most widely used neuron modeling tool is NEURON, originally developed by Michael Hines and John Moore at Duke University in the 1980s and later maintained and expanded at Yale University. NEURON was based on the biophysical equations derived by Alan Hodgkin and Andrew Huxley in 1952 to describe the propagation of electrical impulses along the membrane of the squid giant axon (Hines & Carnevale, 1997). The Hodgkin-Huxley equations describe with remarkable precision how ion channels open and close in response to changes in electrical potential, generating action potentials, which are the fundamental unit of neural communication.

NEURON translates these equations into software, allowing researchers to create detailed models of individual neurons with branched dendrites, varying ion channel densities in different compartments, and realistic synaptic inputs, and simulate their electrical behavior over time. In a sense, it's a virtual electrophysiology lab: a laboratory where researchers can ask what happens to a neuron's firing pattern if they block a specific ion channel or strengthen a synapse, without touching a single living cell.

GENERAL NEural SIMUlation System

The next attempt came from GENESIS (GENERAL NEural SIMUlation System, http://genesis-sim.org/) which was developed by James Bower and David Beeman at the California Institute of Technology (Caltech) in the 1980s as a parallel tool with similar goals: realistic biophysical modeling of neurons with detailed compartmental structure (Bower & Beeman, 1998). For decades, NEURON and GENESIS were the two dominant platforms in the field, each accumulating extensive libraries of published models and communities of researchers who had spent years studying their respective architectures.

According to the 2017 metric (Tikidji-Hamburyan et al., 2017), most commonly used to assess adoption in computational neuroscience, the number of

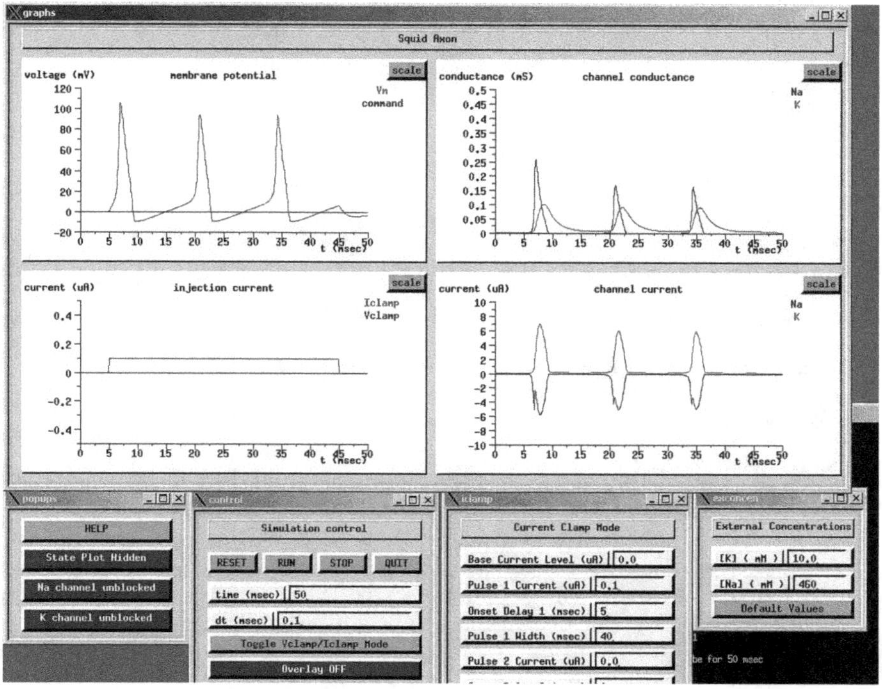

Figure 6.12 A screenshot of the GENESIS interface illustrating the graphical modeling environment for constructing biophysically detailed neural models

Source: Reproduced from Bower, J. M., GENESIS Project (http://www.genesis-sim.org/GENESIS/genesis-cygwin/, used under GPL/LGPL, Wikipedia).

models deposited in Yale's ModelDB database NEURON accounts for approximately 74% of all publicly available models, making it clearly the dominant tool. GENESIS accounts for approximately 5%. These figures are useful because they paint a fair picture of the field: there is one core tool and several important but less widely used alternatives.

Brian

A more modern Brian, created by Romain Brett and Dan Goodman in 2008 and now in its second major version, has adhered to a different design philosophy from the outset. While NEURON and GENESIS require users to learn specialized domain-specific languages to define new neuron models, Brian is written entirely in Python and allows researchers to define models by writing their equations directly in standard mathematical notation just as a theorist would write them on a blackboard.

Brian then automatically generates optimized compiled code in the background. This speeds up the prototyping of new ideas and makes it much more accessible to researchers who are primarily theoreticians rather than software engineers (Goodman & Brette, 2008).

```
from brian import *
eqs = '''
dV/dt  = (ge+gi-(V+49*mV))/(20*ms) : volt
dge/dt = -ge/(5*ms)                : volt
dgi/dt = -gi/(10*ms)               : volt
'''
P = NeuronGroup(4000, model=eqs,
        threshold=-50*mV, reset=-60*mV)
Pe = P.subgroup(3200)
Pi = P.subgroup(800)
Ce = Connection(Pe, P, 'ge')
Ci = Connection(Pi, P, 'gi')
Ce.connect_random(Pe, P, p=0.02,
                  weight=1.62*mV)
Ci.connect_random(Pi, P, p=0.02,
                  weight=-9*mV)
M = SpikeMonitor(P)
P.V = -60*mV+10*mV*rand(len(P))
run(.5*second)
raster_plot(M)
show()
```

$$\tau_m \frac{\mathrm{d}V}{\mathrm{d}t} = -(V - E_L) + g_e + g_i$$

$$\tau_e \frac{\mathrm{d}g_e}{\mathrm{d}t} = -g_e$$

$$\tau_i \frac{\mathrm{d}g_i}{\mathrm{d}t} = -g_i$$

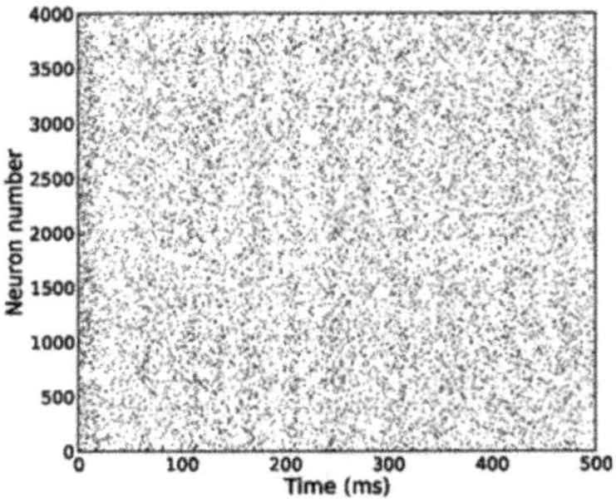

Figure 6.13 Neuron model equations and raster plot in Brian Software
Source: Reproduced from Goodman and Brette (2008) under the terms of the Creative Commons Attribution 4.0 International License, CC BY 4.0.

NEST

While Brian lowered the barrier for theorists to prototype spiking networks in Python, the field was simultaneously moving in the opposite direction as well, toward ever-larger, high-performance simulations, exemplified by NEST. NEST, a neural modeling tool, was developed by Markus Diesmann and his colleagues at the Jülich Research Center in Germany and serves a different niche: modeling very large networks comprising millions of neurons, designed to run efficiently on parallel computing clusters and supercomputers. NEST has become the flagship simulator of the European Human Brain Project, a ten-year, one-billion-euro initiative aimed at modeling the human brain (Gewaltig & Diesmann, 2007).

It's important to be honest about what these tools are and aren't. NEURON, GENESIS, Brian, and NEST are computational neuroscience research platform tools for testing hypotheses, studying the behavior of neural circuits, and building models constrained by experimental data. Researchers using this software published thousands of papers, advanced our understanding of how neurons compute, and enabled researchers to test ideas that would otherwise be impossible to explore in living tissue. But none of them are brain simulations. The models they employ are inevitably simplified: they employ idealized models of neurons with far less biological detail than a real cell, they simulate circuits of thousands or at most millions of neurons rather than billions, and the parameters in these models are set by researchers making educated guesses based on experimental data rather than direct measurements of the actual brain being simulated. They are useful fictions—deliberate simplifications intended to clarify specific questions, not exact replicas intended to reproduce all cognitive processes.

Virtual Steps to the Brain

If these earlier platforms provided increasingly powerful but still abstracted laboratories for testing neural hypotheses, the next step was more ambitious: building personalized, whole-brain simulations grounded directly in an individual's anatomical data, an approach embodied by The Virtual Brain.

The Virtual Brain project was founded in 2008 by Victor Jirsa of Aix-Marseille University, Randy McIntosh of Baycrest in Toronto, and Petra Ritter of Charité Berlin, who heads the brain modeling section there (https://www.thevirtualbrain.org/).

The project received approximately €17 million in funding, primarily from the James S. McDonnell Foundation, and was integrated into the European digital research infrastructure EBRAINS as part of the Human Brain Project (https://ebrains.eu/). By 2018, The Virtual Brain software had already been installed more than 10,000 times.

More importantly, the framework has demonstrated real clinical value: it is the simulator used in EPINOV (https://ins-amu.fr/epinov), a prospective clinical trial evaluating predictive whole-brain modeling to improve epilepsy surgery outcomes (Wang et al., 2023). In this approach, surgeons use a personalized virtual brain model constructed from each patient's structural and diffusion MRI together with intracranial EEG data to simulate seizure propagation and identify candidate regions for resection while minimizing the risk of post-operative cognitive impairment.

As whole-brain modeling efforts expanded and required shared infrastructure, they became embedded within broader European initiatives, most notably EBRAINS, which emerged from the larger and more controversial Human Brain Project.

EBRAINS, the European digital research infrastructure hosting Virtual Brain and other simulation tools, grew out of the Human Brain Project, an initiative announced in 2013 with enormous ambitions and, for a time, considerable controversy. The Human Brain Project was selected by the European Commission as one of two flagship projects in the field of future and emerging technologies, along with the Graphene Research Initiative, and received one billion euros over ten years. Its initial stated goal to simulate an entire human brain on a computer within ten years was met with skepticism by much of the neuroscience community, and not without reason (https://www.humanbrainproject.eu/en/).

In 2014, more than 750 neuroscientists signed an open letter threatening to boycott the project due to concerns about its scientific management and the decision to focus primarily on large-scale modeling at the expense of fundamental neuroscience research. This dispute led to a significant restructuring of the project (Frégnac & Laurent, 2014).

By the time the Human Brain Project concluded in 2023, its most significant legacy is the EBRAINS platform itself—an open research platform that remains available to scientists worldwide and the modeling tools developed on top of it, rather than anything approaching a full-fledged brain simulation (Human Brain Project, 2023).

The Virtual Brain: A Simulator of Primate Brain Network Dynamics

Against this backdrop of ambitious infrastructure-building and tempered expectations, The Virtual Brain stands as a concrete example of what large-scale brain modeling can realistically achieve when it focuses on network dynamics rather than attempting a neuron-by-neuron reconstruction of the entire brain.

The Virtual Brain (TVB) simulator was developed as a unified platform for modeling large-scale network dynamics in the primate brain, combining biologically based models of neuronal mass with empirically derived structural connectivity. Founded by Victor Jirsa (Aix-Marseille University), Randy McIntosh (Baycrest Center for Brain Research), and Petra Ritter (Charité—University Hospital Berlin), the TVB project aims to bridge the gap between detailed neural measurements and whole-brain functional dynamics by creating personalized brain network simulations based on individual structural and functional neuroimaging data.

Unlike detailed simulators of individual neurons, such as NEURON or NEST, TVB focuses on the macroscopic behavior of the network rather than microscopic cellular details. Thus, it serves as a tool for studying how large-scale structural architecture shapes emergent neural dynamics, making it useful for both fundamental neuroscience and potential clinical applications. TVB is integrated into broader research infrastructures such as EBRAINS and has been applied in studies of epilepsy, cognitive disorders, and brain stimulation paradigms, emphasizing its value as a bridge between data and theory, rather than as a literal simulation of every neuron in the brain.

In their paper, Sanz-Leon and colleagues (Sanz-Leon et al., 2013) describe TVB as a computational platform for modeling the spatiotemporal dynamics of large-scale brain networks, reproducing phenomena such as oscillatory activity, synchronization, and perturbations in cortical and subcortical regions. TVB uses neuronal mass models simplified mathematical descriptions of neuronal populations constrained by individual anatomical connectivity (e.g., diffusion MRI tractography) to simulate dynamic brain states that can be compared with empirical functional imaging data.

Whole-brain emulation is based on the idea that if we can capture the brain's complete structure and function, we can reproduce its behavior on a computational substrate. This involves not only mapping neurons and synapses, as discussed in connectomics, but also simulating their electrical and chemical activity in software.

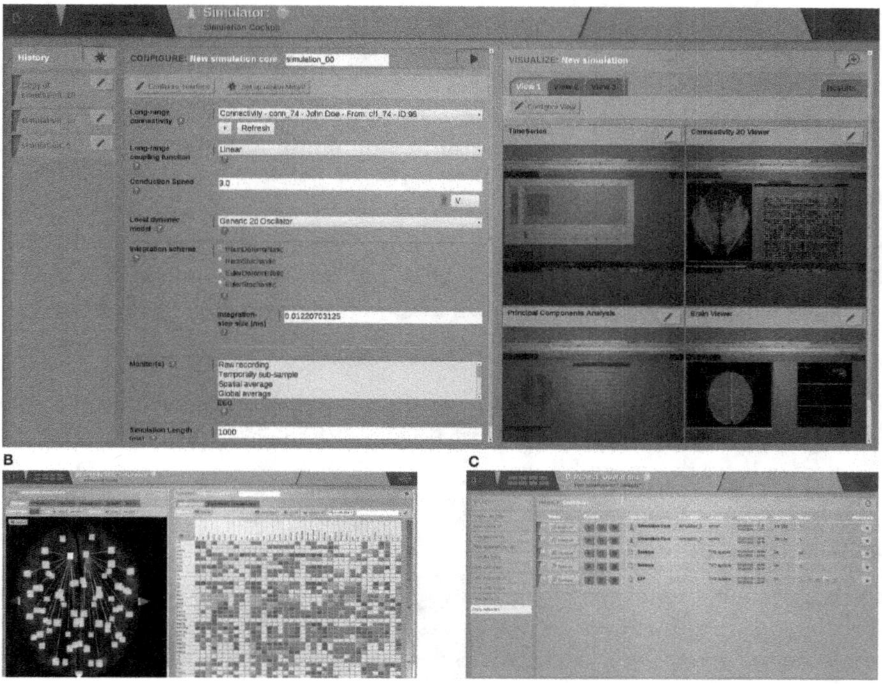

Figure 6.14 The Virtual Brain Simulation Workflow
Source: Adapted from Sanz-Leon et al. (2013) under the terms of the Creative Commons Attribution 3.0 License, CC BY 3.0.

Other Experiments

While the previous sections of the book establish a structural blueprint for the brain through connectomics, brain–computer interface (BCI) experiments provide functional proof of concept that neural activity can be decoded and integrated with computational systems, representing a necessary first step in bridging the gap between biological identity and digital existence.

Elon Musk's Neuralink project aims to achieve high scale in BCI using ultrathin electrodes implanted in the brain, with goals of treating neurological disorders such as stroke and Parkinson's disease and exploring cognitive enhancement. Complementing this effort, Synchron has developed a minimally invasive BCI called the Stentrode, implanted via the vascular system, allowing motor-impaired patients to control digital devices without open brain surgery (Capoot, 2024). In 2025, MergeLab was founded by OpenAI co-founder Sam Altman to advance BCI research using noninvasive technology, focusing on safe, wearable BCIs that can monitor and modulate neural activity without surgery, with applications ranging from cognitive enhancement to neurorehabilitation.

These experiments offer a glimpse of what might be possible in the future—direct BCIs that will expand cognitive abilities beyond biological limitations.

In addition to Neuralink, numerous laboratories are experimenting with BCIs in humans and animals. For example:

- Motor prosthetics: Electrodes in the motor areas of the cerebral cortex allow paralyzed patients to control robotic limbs, restoring lost autonomy (Willsey et al., 2025).
- Sensory prosthetics: Implants in the visual or auditory cortex can create rudimentary "artificial vision" or improve hearing (Trouillet et al., 2025).
- Closed-loop neuromodulation: Devices can monitor neural activity in real time and provide precise stimulation to treat epilepsy, depression, or chronic pain (Ferrero et al., 2025).

These experiments illustrate a key principle: the brain can be manipulated, expanded, and even partially replicated using technology, albeit always under limited and strictly controlled conditions.

Alternative Approaches and Next Steps

Perhaps to understand consciousness we need to go beyond AI and the human brain and turn to nature itself. In Metazoa, Peter Godfrey-Smith (2020) traces the evolutionary roots of consciousness in the animal kingdom. He argues that innovations such as spatially oriented eyes and bodies capable of interacting with the environment were key milestones in the development of subjective experience. Mapping the evolutionary paths of species, from glass sponges to octopuses and primates, Godfrey-Smith connects biological structure with the emergence of mind. While the question of how consciousness emerges from matter remains unanswered, the direction is right.

Clearly, it is far more productive to master small, manageable systems before attempting to mimic the full complexity of the human brain. By deciphering the "birth" of consciousness in simpler organisms, we will finally be able to understand what consciousness truly is and pinpoint the moment of its first appearance.

The history of connectomics, BCIs, and whole-brain emulation clearly demonstrates that scientific progress is built on both failures and breakthroughs. Every obstacle exposes the limits of our tools, models, and sometimes even our assumptions. But these difficulties don't halt progress; they only enhance it.

Moving forward requires patience and consistent, incremental advances. As science advances, collaboration becomes increasingly important. No single discipline can hope to unravel the mysteries of consciousness. Neuroscience, AI, computer engineering, molecular biology, ethics, and philosophy must work together, each contributing to the overall picture. Even the references in this chapter suggest that major advances are occurring right now, with a significant number of papers published in 2025.

Even in last few years, significant progress has been made: from the creation of high-resolution atlases of the human brain to the study of complete systemic connectomes of small animals. These achievements lay the foundation for future developments. Slowly but surely, experiment by experiment, science is paving the way to a deeper understanding of consciousness and, perhaps, eventually, to its preservation.

References

Allen Institute. (2003, September 16). Paul G. Allen commits $100 million to brain research. https://alleninstitute.org/news/paul-g-allen-commits-100-million-to-brain-research/

Berg, S., et al. (2025). Sexual dimorphism in the complete connectome of the Drosophila male central nervous system (bioRxiv preprint, 10.1101/2025.10.09.680999v2). *bioRxiv*. doi:10.1101/2025.10.09.680999v2

Bosch, C., Aidukas, T., Holler, M. et al. (2025). Nondestructive X-ray tomography of brain tissue ultrastructure. *Nat Methods*, 22, 2631–2638. doi:10.1038/s41592-025-02891-0

Bower, J. M., & Beeman, D. (1998). *The Book of GENESIS: Exploring realistic neural models with the GEneral NEural SImulation system* (2nd ed.). Springer-Verlag.

Brenner, S. (1963). *Letter to Max Perutz*. Sydney Brenner Collection, Cold Spring Harbor Laboratory Archives

Capoot, A. (2024, July 30). Neuralink rival Synchron's brain implant now lets people control Apple's Vision Pro with their minds. *CNBC*. https://www.cnbc.com/2024/07/30/neuralink-rival-synchron-offers-thought-control-with-apple-vision-pro-.html

Corrigan, E. K., DeBerardine, M., Poddar, A. et al. (2025). Conservation and alteration of mammalian striatal interneurons. *Nature*, 647, 187–193. doi:10.1038/s41586-025-09592-w

Ding, S.-L., et al. (2016). Comprehensive cellular-resolution atlas of the adult human brain. *Journal of Comparative Neurology*, 524(16), 3127–3481. doi:10.1002/cne.24080

Ferrero, J. J., Hassan, A. R., Yu, Z. et al. (2025). Closed-loop electrical stimulation prevents focal epilepsy progression and long-term memory impairment. *Nat Neurosci*, 28, 1753–1762. doi:10.1038/s41593-025-01988-1

Frégnac, Y., & Laurent, G. (2014). Neuroscience: Where is the brain in the Human Brain Project? *Nature*, 513, 27–29.

Gao, Y., van Velthoven, C. T. J., Lee, C. et al. (2025). Continuous cell-type diversification in mouse visual cortex development. *Nature*, 647, 127–142. doi:10.1038/s41586-025-09644-1

Gewaltig, M.-O., & Diesmann, M. (2007). NEST (NEural Simulation Tool). *Scholarpedia*, 2(4), 1430. doi:10.4249/scholarpedia.1430

Glasser, M., Smith, S., Marcus, D. et al. (2016). The Human Connectome Project's neuroimaging approach. *Nat Neurosci*, 19, 1175–1187. doi:10.1038/nn.4361

Godfrey-Smith, P. (2020). *Metazoa: Animal life and the birth of the mind*. Farrar Straus & Giroux.

Goodman, D. F. M., & Brette, R. (2008). Brian: A simulator for spiking neural networks in Python. *Frontiers in Neuroinformatics*, 2, 5. doi:10.3389/neuro.11.005.2008

Goyal, S., Roumelioti, M. E., Ozga, A. K., & Bloom, J. S. (2020). Carbon-source-dependent metabolism and the survival of the fittest. *Cell*, 181(5), 1112–1124. doi:10.1016/j.cell.2020.04.017

Hagmann, P. (2005). *From diffusion MRI to brain connectomics* [Doctoral dissertation, University of Lausanne].

Herper, M. (2012, March 21). Billionaire Paul G. Allen pours $300 million into quest to find the essence of humanity in the brain. *Forbes*. https://www.forbes.com/sites/matthewherper/2012/03/21/billionaire-paul-g-allen-donates-300-million-in-brain-research-to-understand-what-makes-us-human/

Hines, M. L., & Carnevale, N. T. (1997). The NEURON simulation environment. *Neural Computation*, 9(6), 1179–1209. doi:10.1162/neco.1997.9.6.1179

Holler, M., Raabe, J., Diaz, A., Guizar-Sicairos, M., Wepf, R., Odstrčil, M., & Menzel, A. (2017). High-resolution non-destructive three-dimensional imaging of integrated circuits. *Nature Methods*, 14, 941–943.

Human Brain Project. (2023, September 28). *Human Brain Project ends: What has been achieved?*https://www.humanbrainproject.eu/en/follow-hbp/news/20230928/human-brain-project-ends-what-has-been-achieved/

Humbel, M., et al. (2024). Cellular-resolution X-ray microtomography of an entire mouse brain (arXiv:2405.13971v1).

Kasture, A. S., Hummel, T., Sucic, S., & Freissmuth, M. (2018). Big lessons from tiny flies: Drosophila melanogaster as a model to explore dysfunction of dopaminergic and serotonergic neurotransmitter systems. *International Journal of Molecular Sciences*, 19 (6), Article 1788. doi:10.3390/ijms19061788

Keefe, M. G., Steyert, M. R. & Nowakowski, T. J. (2025). Lineage-resolved atlas of the developing human cortex. *Nature*, 647, 194–202. doi:10.1038/s41586-025-09033-8

MacDonald, F. (2017, December 11). Scientists put a worm brain in a Lego robot body – and it worked. *ScienceAlert*. https://www.sciencealert.com/scientists-put-worm-brain-in-lego-robot-openworm-connectome

National Human Genome Research Institute. (n.d.). 1911: Fruit flies illuminate the chromosome theory. *Genome.gov*. https://www.genome.gov/25520245/online-education-kit-1911-fruit-flies-illuminate-the-chromosome-theory

Rubin, G. M. (2006). Janelia Farm: A new research campus of the Howard Hughes Medical Institute. *Proceedings of the National Academy of Sciences*, 103(44), 15711–15712. https://www.sciencedirect.com/science/article/pii/S0092867406004430

Sanz-Leon, P., Knock, S. A., Woodman, M. M., Domide, L., Mersmann, J., McIntosh, A. R., & Jirsa, V. (2013). The Virtual Brain: A simulator of primate brain network dynamics. *Frontiers in Neuroinformatics*, 7, Article 10. doi:10.3389/fninf.2013.00010

Scheffer, L. K., et al. (2020). A connectome and analysis of the adult Drosophila central brain. *eLife*, 9, e57443. doi:10.7554/eLife.57443

Schlegel, P., Yin, Y., Bates, A. S., Dorkenwald, S., Eichler, K., Jefferis, G. S. X. E., & Murthy, M. (2024). Whole-brain annotation and multi-connectome cell typing of Drosophila. *Nature*, 634(8032), 139–152. doi:10.1038/s41586-024-07686-5

Seung, S. (2010). I am my connectome [Video]. *TED Conferences*. https://www.ted.com/talks/sebastian_seung_i_am_my_connectome

Seung, S. (2013). *Connectome: How the brain's wiring makes us who we are*. Penguin.

Sporns, O., Tononi, G., & Kötter, R. (2005). The human connectome: A structural description of the human brain. *PLoS Computational Biology*, 1(4), Article e42. doi:10.1371/journal.pcbi.0010042

Sterling, A. (2025, March 31). Announcing EyeWire II. *EyeWire Blog*. https://blog.eyewire.org/announcing-eyewire-ii/

Szigeti, B., Gleeson, P., Vella, M., Khayrulin, S., Palyanov, A., Hokanson, J., Currie, M., Cantarelli, M., Idili, G., & Larson, S. (2014). OpenWorm: An open-science approach to modeling Caenorhabditis elegans. *Frontiers in Computational Neuroscience*, 8, Article 137. doi:10.3389/fncom.2014.00137

The Nobel Assembly at the Karolinska Institutet. (2002). *The Nobel Prize in Physiology or Medicine 2002: Sydney Brenner, H. Robert Horvitz & John E. Sulston — for their discoveries concerning genetic regulation of organ development and programmed cell death* (Press release). NobelPrize.org.

Tikidji-Hamburyan, R. A., Narayana, V., Bozkus, Z., & El-Ghazawi, T. A. (2017). Software for brain network simulations: A comparative study. *Frontiers in Neuroinformatics*, 11, Article 46. doi:10.3389/fninf.2017.00046

Trouillet, A., Revol, E., Coen, F. V. et al. (2025). High-resolution prosthetic hearing with a soft auditory brainstem implant in macaques. *Nat. Biomed. Eng*, 9, 1403–1417. doi:10.1038/s41551-025-01378-9

Wang, H. E., Woodman, M. M., Triebkorn, P., Lemarechal, J. D., Jha, J., Giusiano, B., Lagarde, S., Bartolomei, F., Benar, C. G., & Jirsa, V. K. (2023). Delineating epileptogenic networks using brain imaging data and personalized modeling in drug-resistant epilepsy. *Science Translational Medicine*, 15(680), Article eabp8982. doi:10.1126/scitranslmed.abp8982

White, J. G., Southgate, E., Thomson, J. N., & Brenner, S. (1986). The structure of the nervous system of the nematode Caenorhabditis elegans. *Philosophical Transactions of the Royal Society of London*. Series B, Biological Sciences, 314(1165), 1–340. doi:10.1098/rstb.1986.0056

Willsey, M. S., Shah, N. P., Avansino, D. T. et al. (2025). A high-performance brain–computer interface for finger decoding and quadcopter game control in an individual with paralysis. *Nat Med*, 31, 96–104. doi:10.1038/s41591-024-03341-8

Xu, C. S. et al. (2020). A connectome of the adult drosophila central brain. *bioRxiv*. doi:10.1101/2020.01.21.911859

Yu, X., Creamer, M. S., Randi, F., Sharma, A. K., Linderman, S. W., & Leifer, A. M. (2021). Fast deep learning correspondence for neuron tracking and identification in C. elegans using synthetic training (preprint). *arXiv*. doi:10.48550/arXiv.2101.08211

Zhao, R., Wang, T., Moon, T. et al. (2025). A spiking artificial neuron based on one diffusive memristor, one transistor and one resistor. *Nat Electron*, 8, 1211–1221. doi:10.1038/s41928-025-01488-x

Zilles, K., & Amunts, K. (2010). Centenary of Brodmann's map — conception and fate. *Nature Reviews Neuroscience*, 11(2), 139–145. doi:10.1038/nrn2776

7 Fears and Dreams of Digital Immortality

Introduction

The preceding chapters trace the development of practical neuroscience from 302 worm neurons to the partial mapping of the human brain, demonstrating both the extraordinary capabilities of modern experimental tools and the vast scope of what remains unexplored. However, progress in the laboratory does not occur in a social or philosophical vacuum. For every published experiment, there is the potential for a parallel dialogue to emerge outside the laboratory between ethicists, policymakers, patients, journalists, and ordinary people who share their own intuitions about identity, mortality, and the limits of science. This chapter addresses this dialogue. It examines the ethical concerns surrounding consciousness transference research, the practical and institutional reasons why progress is slower than often suggested in the popular literature, the persistent problem of pseudoscience, and the future directions most likely to lead to genuine discoveries. It concludes with a broader reflection on the nature of scientific breakthroughs and why predicting them is perhaps the most difficult problem of all.

When Science Contradicts Itself: Public Attitudes and Ethical Debates

Despite the impressive scientific progress described in the previous chapters, mind uploading remains a controversial ethical topic in contemporary research. This debate is more than just a philosophical abstraction; it impacts funding decisions, the regulatory environment, and the degree of freedom researchers have to publish and collaborate. To understand why so many people, including many scientists themselves, feel genuinely uneasy, it's necessary to go beyond the technical literature and engage with the psychology and moral philosophy that shape public reaction.

One of the most revealing empirical contributions to this debate is a 2018 study by Michael Laakasuo and colleagues, which examined what actually predicts approval or disapproval of mind uploading technology among the general public (Laakasuo et al., 2018).

The results were counterintuitive. One might expect support for such technology to correlate with scientific literacy, analytical thinking ability, or

DOI: 10.4324/9781003794677-8

familiarity with neuroscience. Laakasuo's study found that none of these factors was a major predictor. Instead, approval or disapproval was largely determined by individual differences in disgust sensitivity, particularly to sexual disgust, and moral attitudes emphasizing purity, as defined by moral foundations theory.

The study revealed several distinct patterns. People who rated purity morality highly, those who view certain actions as inherently defiling or polluting, regardless of their consequences, were significantly more likely to express disapproval of consciousness transfer technology. In contrast, exposure to science fiction proved to be a strong positive predictor: people who had read a lot of fiction about consciousness transfer were more open to the idea, presumably because exposure to the narrative normalized the concept and encouraged them to consider its implications from a safe, imaginary distance. Notably, people who rated fear of death highly were not more opposed to consciousness transfer; on the contrary, they tended to be more accepting, viewing the technology as a potential life-extender rather than an affront to it. A particularly striking result was that the nature of the target platform, whether the transferred consciousness would reside in a computer, an android body, or an artificial biological brain, had no significant impact on moral judgments. The act of movement itself, rather than the destination, was what caused moral concern (Laakasuo et al., 2023).

These findings help explain why the ethical debate surrounding consciousness transference so often unfolds at cross-purposes. Critics and proponents often misunderstand each other, responding to fundamentally different issues. Opponents, who base their objections on moral intuitions based on principles of purity, are unlikely to be convinced by technical evidence of the informational completeness of transference or philosophical arguments about personal identity. Their objection is largely moral, rooted in an emotional dimension that logic cannot easily grasp. Proponents, by contrast, may be frustrated by what they perceive as irrational resistance to life-extension technology. Understanding the psychological structure of these opposing positions is not merely academically interesting; it is a prerequisite for any productive public discussion of how such research should be regulated.

Beyond public opinion, there remains a persistent ethical tension within the scientific community itself. Many researchers contributing to neuroscience, brain–computer interfaces (BFIs), or computer modeling simultaneously experience ambivalence about the direction their work will ultimately lead. The concerns expressed are varied. As mentioned earlier, there were also controversies surrounding the Human Brain Project, for which the European Union allocated €1 billion to create a complete digital model of the human brain. However, hundreds of leading neuroscientists soon criticized the direction of the work (Webb, 2014).

Why Progress Is Slower Than It Appears: Practical and Institutional Constraints

Popular science journalism often creates the impression that breakthroughs in neuroscience and artificial intelligence (AI) are happening one after another, and that the gap between laboratory discoveries and revolutionary technologies is narrowing with each passing year. In some fields, this is indeed true. BCIs capable of deciphering the speech of paralyzed patients, highly accurate mapping of the connectome of small organisms, and AI systems that detect patterns in neural data at a speed unmatched by any human researcher all represent genuine and recent advances (Littlejohn et al., 2025). However, the gap between these advances and anything resembling mind uploading remains vast, and to understand the reasons for this, it's necessary to address limitations that rarely make headlines.

- The first technological limitation is biological complexity. Chapter 5 of the book is devoted to this.
- Secondly, there is an ethical framework governing experiments on living neural tissue. The most direct path to understanding how consciousness arises and what is required to transmit it involves experimental manipulation of the human brain under controlled conditions, an approach that is rightly prohibited. Therefore, the vast majority of invasive neuroscience research is conducted on animal models: rodents, primates, and invertebrates.
- Third, the international regulatory framework for neuroscience research is fragmented and inconsistent. What is permitted in one jurisdiction may be prohibited in another. Protocols for processing neural data, which contain intimate personal information and raise serious privacy concerns, vary significantly across countries. International collaboration, which is increasingly necessary given the scale of resources required for projects like whole-brain mapping, must overcome these regulatory gaps at every turn. As a result, promising research programs may be delayed or forced to pursue suboptimal projects not because of any scientific failures, but because of the difficulty of reaching cross-border ethical consensus.

Science and Pseudoscience, Misinformation, and the Challenge of Clarity

The intersection of consciousness research, AI, and the prospect of digital immortality has proven irresistible to a particular brand of entrepreneurial optimism, an optimism that, at its least responsible, devolves into pseudoscience and deliberate misinformation. This is no minor issue. In an information environment where AI-generated content can replicate plausible-sounding scientific claims on a large scale, and where the emotional component of mortality research guarantees a large audience for dramatic claims, the ability to distinguish genuine science from staged material has become a crucial skill for any interested reader.

Where should the line between science and pseudoscience be drawn? Does institutional affiliation guarantee scientific legitimacy? In 2018, the startup Nectome made headlines with a presentation that sounded unusual, to say the least: they promised to preserve your brain in such high detail that it could one day be "uploaded" into a computer, but there was a catch. For best results, the brain had to be "fresh."

- In effect, the procedure required preservation immediately following death, raising profound ethical concerns. Nectome marketed the service as a form of "physician-assisted euthanasia" aimed at people with terminal illnesses (Hern, 2018).
- Consequences: The Massachusetts Institute of Technology (MIT) Media Lab, which collaborated with Nectome, faced widespread public outrage. Critics accused the startup of selling "commercialized suicide" based on science that didn't yet exist. MIT ultimately severed ties, claiming that the scientific premise of "uploading" was far from reality (TechCrunch, 2018).

The hallmarks of pseudoscience in this field follow familiar patterns. Extraordinary claims are made without reference to peer-reviewed scientific data. Vague but powerful phrases, "soul uploading," "digital resurrection," "consciousness preserved forever", replace technical precision. Commercial interests are presented as research programs; fundraising announcements are couched in the language of scientific achievement. Chronological timelines are presented with a confidence that no honest researcher would endorse. These tendencies are not unique to consciousness research; they appear wherever the gap between scientific possibilities and public desire is wide, but they are particularly pronounced here, as the associated desire (to avoid death) is one of the strongest that people experience.

This doesn't mean that all grandiose claims in this field are fraudulent. Genuine scientific discoveries are sometimes accompanied by claims that resemble hype. The challenge is to develop critical evaluation skills that distinguish between these two approaches. Several practical heuristics are useful. Is the claim published in a peer-reviewed journal or announced via a press release or crowdfunding campaign? Are the researchers affiliated with established academic or research institutions, or do they work entirely outside of this infrastructure? Does the claim describe a specific, verifiable discovery or contain general promises about future possibilities? Do independent experts in the relevant fields express cautious enthusiasm or sharp skepticism? None of these heuristics is infallible, but together they provide a reasonable filter against the most egregious cases of misinformation.

The Head Transplant Debate: When Scientists Disagree on What Is Possible

An even more dramatic example of speculative neuroscience entering the public arena is the debate over head transplantation. Perhaps no recent episode in the history of interdisciplinary neuroscience has attracted as much public attention or as much scientific controversy as the purported head transplant experiments involving Italian neurosurgeon Sergio Canavero and his Chinese colleague Xiaoping Ren. In 2017, Ren announced a head transplant on a human cadaver at Harbin Medical University, claiming it demonstrated the surgical feasibility of repairing damaged spinal cords. Canavero had for years publicized his quest to perform the first head transplant on a living human, sparking a massive media outcry and heated debate about the ethics and scientific validity of the undertaking.

The reaction from the scientific community was largely dismissive. Neurosurgeons, primarily working in this field, pointed out that the core problem of repairing a damaged spinal cord in a living patient in a way that restores meaningful neural function remained unsolved, and that performing the procedure on a cadaver meant nothing about its viability in a living person. The claim that a chemical compound called polyethylene glycol (PEG) could reconnect severed axons was disputed on both theoretical and empirical levels. No peer-reviewed evidence was presented of restoration of sensory or motor function by reconnecting the spinal cord. Most experts considered this episode an example of speculative surgical ambitions being promoted as scientific progress (Burnett, 2017).

Nevertheless, the controversy was not without scientific merit. It sparked a public debate about questions truly central to the long-term project of understanding the brain–body connection: What would it mean for a person's identity if their brain were in another body? Would the person who underwent such a procedure be the same person as the one who underwent it? How does the brain–body connection, the hormonal environment, proprioceptive feedback, and immune signals, influence what we perceive as self? These questions cannot be resolved by the head transplant experiments that have been conducted, but they are real questions, and this episode served as an opportunity to elevate them to a broader public agenda. The fact that a bold and dubious claim has provoked serious philosophical and scientific reflection is no argument in favor of the claim; it's a reminder that even failed or falsified experiments can have productive intellectual side effects.

Plausible Future Scenarios and False Promises

Among the many visions for the future of neuroscience and AI, some are more realistic than others. To determine which future claims deserve serious consideration as opposed to skeptical dismissal, it's important to understand which problems are fundamentally solvable and which depend on theoretical breakthroughs that may occur decades or centuries in the future.

Medium-term prospects that enjoy genuine scientific consensus are relatively modest compared to the most grandiose visions of consciousness transfer. BCIs will almost certainly continue to improve, enabling increasingly precise communication between neural signals and external devices. Partial simulations of specific cognitive circuit models of memory consolidation in the hippocampus, decision-making in the prefrontal cortex, and sensory processing pathways will become more accurate and useful as both imaging technologies and computational methods advance. Therapeutic applications of neurotechnology, from closed-loop stimulation systems for handling treatment-resistant depression to prosthetic sensory systems for patients with blindness or deafness, are already moving from the research stage into clinical practice.

The integration of AI and neuroscience deserves special attention as a source of real progress in the near future. Machine learning algorithms trained on large neural data sets are already capable of identifying patterns in brain activity that no human analyst could detect on their own. They can predict with astonishing accuracy which neurons are active during specific cognitive states, decipher predicted motor movements from cortical signals, and detect early signs of neurodegenerative diseases in imaging data. As these tools become increasingly powerful and widely used, they will accelerate progress in several areas of neuroscience, not by solving the complex problem of consciousness, but by creating the empirical foundations on which a future theoretical solution can be built.

What currently doesn't seem convincing are any firm timelines for full consciousness uploading, digital immortality, or the preservation of individual consciousness in computational form. The obstacles aren't just technical; they're conceptual. We don't yet know which aspects of neural organization encode the subjective qualities of experience, and until we do, we won't be able to reliably reproduce them. Claims promising such capabilities within decades should be treated with considerable skepticism, regardless of the qualifications of those making them. This isn't pessimism, but epistemological honesty. The history of consciousness research is rife with premature overconfidence, and the field has, albeit slowly, realized that the problem is much deeper than it first appears.

Digital Twins of the Mind

One concept that has gained traction in both scientific research and commercial contexts is the idea of a "digital twin," a computational model of human cognitive processes detailed enough to simulate their reactions to new situations, predict their behavioral tendencies, or serve as a substitute for medical decisions.

This term is borrowed from engineering, where digital twins of physical systems, such as aircraft engines, power grids, and manufacturing processes, are routinely used to model performance and predict failures. The question is whether a similar approach can be meaningfully applied to the human mind.

Early examples of this idea already exist in the form of AI-powered chatbots for creating memorials and personalization systems. These systems can reproduce stylistic patterns from a person's digital communications, answer questions based on their documented opinions, and simulate behavioral tendencies based on historical data. The most commercially successful versions of digital twins use years of text messages, emails, social media posts, and recorded speech to build probabilistic models of how a given person is likely to respond in different conversational contexts.

However, modern digital twins of this kind are not based on neural data. They are language models, not thought models. This distinction is important. A language model trained on a person's communications can reproduce how that person expressed themselves; it cannot reproduce how they thought, felt, or perceived the world. Confusion between these two concepts is one of the fallacies in discussions of digital immortality.

Biointegrated Data and the Future of Digital Immortality

Yet language-based replication is only the beginning. The next frontier of digital immortality goes far beyond chatbots that mimic a person's communication style. Today's AI can analyze messages, emails, social media posts, and recorded speech to simulate how someone might respond in conversation. But to create a more faithful digital twin, a virtual continuation of a person, future systems will need to integrate not just behavioral history, but also biometric and neural data collected over time.

Wearable devices like smartwatches already track heart rate, sleep patterns, activity, and stress. Future devices, including EEG-enabled headphones or other noninvasive BCIs, could add neural signals to the mix. By combining these streams, a digital twin could not only reproduce a person's communication style, but also capture patterns in thought, mood, and cognitive states, creating a richer and more personalized model of the individual.

This integration reflects a key insight: cognition and identity are deeply intertwined with the body. Emotions, decision-making, memory, and attention are influenced by hormonal cycles, autonomic nervous system activity, and metabolic states. Ignoring these signals limits how accurately a digital twin can model the living person. Including them moves us closer to a system that might, in principle, simulate not only what a person says, but also how they think and feel—a step toward digital continuity of identity.

However, even perfect behavioral and neural recording does not logically guarantee identity preservation. It may enable:

- Predictive modelling.
- High-fidelity simulation.
- Behavioral continuity.

But identity is not clearly reducible to pattern replication, of course, and these possibilities raise serious ethical and privacy questions. Continuous monitoring of brain and body data reveals intimate aspects of cognition, emotion, and intention. Any project aiming for digital immortality must confront these issues head-on: how to protect personal data, respect consent, and define what it means to preserve a "self" in digital form.

When the Impossible Becomes Obvious

Stepping back from these technical possibilities, we arrive at a deeper question. What's most striking about consciousness is this: we live with it from the moment we're born. Because it's always present, because it's inseparable from our experience of existence, we rarely stop to question it. Just as gravity pulls us toward the Earth every second of our lives, consciousness pulls us toward itself, toward the experience of being someone, of perceiving, feeling, and knowing. And yet, both remain mysterious. We treat them as obvious facts of existence, though they are among the deepest unsolved problems in all of science. For millennia, gravity simply "was." People accepted it without asking what it consisted of or why it behaved the way it did. Even today, we describe gravity with extremely precise equations, but not with a definitive metaphysical explanation.

Consciousness is also present to us in every thought, every perception, every feeling, and we still cannot satisfactorily explain how the physical processes of the brain even give rise to experience.

This book attempts to show that the difficulty of understanding the mind lies not so much in the absence of advanced technology, although technology plays a huge role. We have made progress in neuroscience, AI, and computational modeling. And yet, the central question posed by ancient philosophers long before the advent of microscopes and MRI machines remains fundamentally unanswered. We find ourselves at a strange moment in history: technology advances, but the mystery of consciousness remains virtually unchanged.

It might be assumed that progress follows a smooth and predictable path, and we should simply wait, but history shows otherwise, with many striking examples. Consider electricity. The ancient Greeks noticed that rubbed amber could attract small objects, a curious phenomenon observed around the sixth century BC. And then, the advent of new knowledge? Nothing. No grand theory, no technological breakthrough, no coordinated research program. For over two thousand years, the world held this little secret in its hands, largely unaware of its significance. This wasn't ignorance in the modern sense; the knowledge existed, but no one understood what it meant. It wasn't until the late sixteenth century that William Gilbert, a physician, not a naturalist by training, began to systematically study electrical and magnetic phenomena. His work laid the foundation for an entirely new understanding of the natural world, and he is credited with coining the word electricity. Gilbert's work marked a decisive turning point after centuries of relative neglect.

This pattern has been repeated throughout the history of science. Faraday, with virtually no formal education, grasped the unity of electricity and magnetism through a combination of physical intuition and tireless experimentation, and it was he who transformed magnetism into electricity. Maxwell's prodigious mind translated Faraday's ideas into mathematical form, creating equations whose implications took decades to understand fully. Edison and Tesla, confronted by contrasting temperaments and incompatible views, together transformed these equations into a technology that transformed civilization. Each of these figures operated in a distinct historical context, with distinct tools and distinct problems. But none of them could have foreseen their own contributions in advance, and none of their contemporaries could have confidently predicted which of the many competing approaches would prove decisive.

Another prime example is the Wright Brothers, who were bicycle mechanics, not professional engineers or scientists. Most educated technical experts of the time considered heavier-than-air flight impossible, or at least not inevitable.

Their success depended not on superior professional skills but on a willingness to approach the problem empirically, building, testing, observing, adjusting, and building again. A few years after Kitty Hawk, aviation became a competitive sport in Europe, with festivals dedicated to new speed and distance records. From the "impossible" to international competition in less than a decade: such is the rhythm of fundamental breakthroughs, when the right combination of vision, determination, and circumstance converges.

The question of when we will understand consciousness, when its neural basis will be fully elucidated, and when the possibility of its preservation or transmission will move from the realm of speculation to the realm of engineering solutions cannot be answered honestly. Technologies map the brain with exquisite precision, accumulate data on a scale that would have seemed unimaginable a generation ago, and create AI systems capable of discovering patterns that no human analyst could have found. And yet, the central understanding we seek may come not from a better tool, but from a better question. Einstein's theory of relativity didn't begin with an expensive apparatus. It began with a thought experiment: what would it be like to drive next to a beam of light? The answer revolutionized physics.

Progress in understanding the mind will almost certainly require both better tools and better ideas, each of which will inform the development of the other. The experiments described in Chapter 6 are not footnotes to a pre-planned history; they are an accumulation of empirical data that future theorists will have to work with. Just as the centuries of careful observation that preceded Newton were not wasted, even though those conducting the observations had no idea what they were looking for. Connectome maps, BCI recordings, partial neural simulations, and modern digital twin models are laying the foundations whose implications we have yet to fully appreciate.

Ultimately, this is cause for cautious optimism, not euphoria or despair. The problem of consciousness is complex, but complex problems have been solved before, often unexpectedly, often by someone no one expected. The only guarantee is that the answer will not come to those who have stopped looking.

References

Burnett, D. (2017). No, there hasn't been a human "head transplant," and there may never be. *The Guardian*. https://www.theguardian.com/science/brain-flapping/2017/nov/17/no-there-hasnt-been-a-human-head-transplant-and-may-never-be-sergio-canavero

Hern, A. (2018). Startup wants to upload your brain to the cloud, but has to kill you to do it. *The Guardian*. https://www.theguardian.com/technology/2018/mar/14/nectome-startup-upload-brain-the-cloud-kill-you

Laakasuo, M., Sundvall, J., & Drosinou, M. (2018). Personal moral views and individual differences in mind uploading attitudes. *Personality and Individual Differences*, 127, 151–160. doi:10.1016/j.paid.2018.01.055

Laakasuo, M., Sundvall, J., Francis, K., Drosinou, M., Hannikainen, I., Kunnari, A., & Palomäki, J. (2023). Would you exchange your soul for immortality?—Existential meaning and afterlife beliefs predict mind upload approval. *Frontiers in Psychology*, 14, Article 1254846. doi:10.3389/fpsyg.2023.1254846

Littlejohn, K. T., Cho, C. J., Liu, J. R. et al. (2025). A streaming brain-to-voice neuroprosthesis to restore naturalistic communication. *Nat Neurosci*, 28, 902–912. doi:10.1038/s41593-025-01905-6

TechCrunch. (2018, April 3). MIT cuts ties with brain preservation startup Nectome. https://techcrunch.com/2018/04/03/mit-cuts-ties-with-nectome/

Webb, J. (2014, July 7). Neuroscientists attack "off-course" human brain project. *BBC News*. https://www.bbc.co.uk/news/science-environment-28193790

Appendix

In the preceding chapters, we explored a wide range of topics related to consciousness, the brain, and digital immortality. However, the scope of progress toward digital mind preservation is far too vast to capture fully in a single volume. A comprehensive treatment of every technical nuance would require an entire library rather than a single book. Nevertheless, the discussion does not end here.

This appendix organizes key references cited throughout the book and presents additional resources that, while not included in the main text, are essential for a deeper understanding of the subject. These resources range from open-access data sets and brain mapping projects to simulation platforms, citizen science initiatives, and cutting-edge research in neuromorphic computing and brain–computer interfaces.

For readers eager to explore hands-on applications, a dedicated GitHub repository has been created by me, featuring scripts and tools for accessing brain data and bridging the gap between theory and practice:

Repository: https://github.com/Consciousness-Is-Measurable

Your suggestions and feedback are welcome and can be submitted via the GitHub repository. Contributions will be considered in future editions of this work.

The following sections provide detailed descriptions and links to projects, data sets, simulations, and papers spanning connectomics, brain simulation, AI ethics, neuroscience, and neurotechnology startups. These resources serve as a gateway for both curious readers and researchers interested in exploring the rapidly evolving landscape of brain science and digital consciousness.

EyeWire

EyeWire is a citizen science game developed at Princeton University's Seung Lab that lets anyone—without a scientific background—help map the three-dimensional structure of neurons. Players solve 3D puzzles to reconstruct retinal neurons, advancing connectomics research and helping to train the AI algorithms used in large-scale brain mapping.

Website: https://eyewire.org/explore
GitHub: https://github.com/seung-lab/eyewire-public-api
YouTube: https://www.youtube.com/EyewireOrg

OpenWorm

OpenWorm is an open-source international project dedicated to creating the first complete computational model of Caenorhabditis elegans (C. elegans)—a microscopic roundworm with exactly 302 neurons. The project simulates the worm's entire nervous system and body mechanics from the bottom up, using tools such as Sibernetic (physics engine) and c302 (neural simulation). All code and data are freely available. OpenWorm is considered a foundational proof-of-concept for whole-organism brain emulation.

Website: https://openworm.org/
GitHub: https://github.com/openworm
YouTube: https://www.youtube.com/OpenWorm
Simulation: http://browser.openworm.org/

Janelia Research Campus—FlyEM/FlyWire

Janelia Research Campus (HHMI) hosts the FlyEM project, which has produced the most complete connectomes of the Drosophila (fruit fly) nervous system to date. In 2024, the FlyWire Consortium published the first full adult female fly brain connectome—140,000 neurons and 50+ million synapses—in Nature. *A male CNS connectome followed, enabling the first sex-comparative connectomics study. These data sets are publicly accessible and already used in over 50 publications. The quote in this book—"not only what is connected, but also why certain connections differ" (Berg et al., 2025)—reflects the questions now opened by this work.*

Janelia Website: https://www.janelia.org/
FlyWire Website: https://flywire.ai/
YouTube: https://www.youtube.com/@flywireprinceton4189

Allen Brain Atlas

The Allen Brain Atlas (Allen Institute for Brain Science) is one of the world's most comprehensive open-access brain mapping resources. It integrates gene expression data, connectivity maps, and neuroanatomical reference atlases across multiple species (mouse, human, macaque). The Allen Brain Cell Atlas now contains transcriptomic data for ~4 million cells and is continuously updated. All data and the Allen SDK are freely available.

Website: https://brain-map.org/
Allen Brain Cell Atlas: https://brain-map.org/bkp/explore/abc-atlas

GitHub (AllenInstitute): https://github.com/AllenInstitute
YouTube: https://www.youtube.com/@AllenInstitute

Human Connectome Project (HCP)

The Human Connectome Project is a large-scale, multi-institutional effort to map the structural and functional connectivity of the healthy adult human brain using multimodal MRI and MEG imaging. It has released data from over 1,200 young adults and now spans lifespan projects (prenatal through 100+) and disease cohorts. All data and open-source tools (Connectome Workbench, HCP Pipelines) are freely distributed. The HCP is widely regarded as the definitive open data set for human neuroimaging.

Website: https://www.humanconnectome.org/
GitHub: https://github.com/humanconnectome

Brain Simulation Platforms

The Virtual Brain (TVB)

The Virtual Brain is a neuroinformatics platform for building and running large-scale brain network simulations. It combines biophysically grounded models of neuronal mass with empirically derived structural connectivity (from DTI scans). TVB is used clinically to predict seizure propagation (EPINOV project) and to test hypotheses about brain dynamics in health and disease. Founded by Victor Jirsa (Aix-Marseille University) and Randy McIntosh.

Website: https://www.thevirtualbrain.org/
Simulation: https://www.thevirtualbrain.org/tvb/zwei/brainsimulator-software
GitHub: https://github.com/the-virtual-brain

EBRAINS/Human Brain Project

EBRAINS is the open research infrastructure of the Human Brain Project (EU), providing access to brain atlases, simulation tools, data sets, and high-performance computing resources for neuroscience.

EBRAINS: https://ebrains.eu/
Human Brain Project: https://www.humanbrainproject.eu/en/
GitHub: https://github.com/humanbrainproject
YouTube: https://www.youtube.com/@TheHumanBrainProject

GENESIS (GEneral NEural SImulation System)

GENESIS is one of the earliest and most widely used platforms for simulating neural circuits at multiple levels of biological detail, from single ion channels to large networks.

Website: http://genesis-sim.org/
Software: http://genesis-sim.org/GENESIS/
GitHub: https://github.com/genesis-sim/genesis-2.4

Suggested Reading

Neuromorphic Computing and Brain Simulation

Allen Institute. (2025, November 17). One of world's most detailed virtual brain simulations is changing how we study the brain. *Allen Institute News*. https://alleninstitute.org/news/one-of-worlds-most-detailed-virtual-brain-simulations-is-changing-how-we-study-the-brain/

Massachusetts Institute of Technology. (2026, January 12). This new tool could tell us how consciousness works. *MIT News*. https://news.mit.edu/2026/new-tool-could-tell-us-how-consciousness-works-0112

Theilman, B. H. & Aimone, J. B. (2025). Solving sparse finite element problems on neuromorphic hardware. *Nat Mach Intell*, 7, 1845–1857. doi:10.1038/s42256-025-01143-2

Philosophy of Mind and Personal Identity

Agar, N. (2010). *Humanity's end: Why we should reject radical enhancement*. MIT Press. https://chooser.crossref.org/?doi=10.7551%2Fmitpress%2F9780262014625.001.0001

Blackmore, S. (2005). *Conversations on consciousness*. Oxford University Press. https://www.amazon.co.uk/Conversations-Consciousness-Minds-Think-about/dp/0195179595

Bostrom, N. (2016). The control problem. In: Schneider, S. (ed.), *Science fiction and philosophy: From time travel to superintelligence* (pp. 308–330). Wiley-Blackwell. doi:10.1002/9781118922590.ch23

Chalmers, D. J. (1996). *The conscious mind* . Oxford University Press. https://psycnet.apa.org/record/1996-97863-000

Metzinger, T. (2013). *The ego tunnel*. Basic Books. https://www.goodreads.com/book/show/5895503

Shoemaker, S. (1984). *Identity, cause, and mind*. Cambridge University Press. https://www.amazon.co.uk/Identity-Cause-Mind-Sydney-Shoemaker/dp/0521318246

AI Ethics and Digital Minds

Bostrom, N. (2003). Are we living in a computer simulation?, *The Philosophical Quarterly*, 53(211), 243–255. doi:10.1111/1467-9213.00309

Bostrom, N., & Yudkowsky, E. (2018). The ethics of artificial intelligence. In: Yampolskiy, R. V. (ed.), *Artificial intelligence safety and security* (pp. 57–69). Chapman & Hall/CRC, Taylor & Francis Group. doi:10.1201/9781351251389-4

Metzinger, T. (2021). Artificial suffering: An argument for a global moratorium on synthetic phenomenology. *Journal of Artificial Intelligence and Consciousness*, 8(1), 43–66. doi:10.1142/S270507852150003X

Schwitzgebel, E. (2015). If materialism is true, the United States is probably conscious. *Philos Stud*, 172, 1697–1721. doi:10.1007/s11098-014-0387-8

Connectomics and Brain Mapping

Helmstaedter, M. (2013). Cellular-resolution connectomics: Challenges of dense neural circuit reconstruction. *Nature Methods*, 10(6), 501–507. https://www.nature.com/articles/nmeth.2476

Lichtman, J. W., & Denk, W. (2011). The big and the small: Challenges of imaging the brain's circuits. *Science*, 334(6056), 618–623. https://www.science.org/doi/10.1126/science.1209168

Seung, S. (2012). *Connectome: How the brain's wiring makes us who we are*. Houghton Mifflin Harcourt.

Sporns, O. (2011). *Networks of the brain*. MIT Press.

Large-Scale Brain Atlases and Human Mapping Projects

Amunts, K., & Zilles, K. (2015). Architectonic mapping of the human brain beyond Brodmann. *Neuron*, 88(6), 1086–1107. doi:10.1016/j.neuron.2015.12.001

Jones, A. R. et al. (2009). The Allen Brain Atlas: 5 years and beyond. *Nature Reviews Neuroscience*, 10, 821–828. doi:10.1038/nrn2722

Van Essen, D. C. et al. (2013). The WU-Minn Human Connectome Project: An overview. *NeuroImage*, 80, 62–79. doi:10.1016/j.neuroimage.2013.05.041

Brain Simulation and Computational Modeling

Deco, G., Jirsa, V., & McIntosh, A. R. (2011). Emerging concepts for the dynamical organization of resting-state activity. *Nature Reviews Neuroscience*, 12, 43–56. doi:10.1038/nrn2961

Eliasmith, C. (2013). *How to build a brain*. Oxford University Press.

Koch, C., & Segev, I. (1998). *Methods in neuronal modeling* (2nd ed.). MIT Press.

Markram, H. (2006). The Blue Brain Project. *Nature Reviews Neuroscience*, 7, 153–160. doi:10.1038/nrn1848

Neuromorphic Engineering and Artificial Neurons

Indiveri, G., & Liu, S.-C. (2015). Memory and information processing in neuromorphic systems. *Proceedings of the IEEE*, 103(8), 1379–1397. doi:10.1109/JPROC.2015.2444094

Mead, C. (2020). How we created neuromorphic engineering. *Nature Electronics*. doi:10.1038/s41928-020-0462-4

Brain–Computer Interfaces and Neuroscience

Bear, M. F., Connors, B. W., & Paradiso, M. A. (2020). *Neuroscience: Exploring the brain* (Enhanced 4th ed.). Jones & Bartlett Learning.

Kandel, E. R., Koester, J. D., Mack, S. H., & Siegelbaum, S. A. (eds). (2021). *Principles of neural science* (6th ed.). McGraw-Hill Education.

Wolpaw, J. R., & Wolpaw, E. W. (eds). (2012). *Brain–computer interfaces: Principles and practice.* Oxford University Press.

Critical and Philosophical Perspectives

Dennett, D. C. (1991). *Consciousness explained.* Little, Brown and Company.

Krakauer, J. W., et al. (2017). Neuroscience needs behavior: Correcting a reductionist bias. *Neuron*, 93(3), 480–490. doi:10.1016/j.neuron.2016.12.041

Evolutionary Origins of Neural Systems

Godfrey-Smith, P. (2016). *Other minds: The octopus, the sea, and the deep origins of consciousness.* Farrar, Straus and Giroux. https://www.goodreads.com/book/show/28116739

Shepherd, G. M. (ed.). (2004). *The synaptic organization of the brain* (5th ed.). Oxford University Press.

Additional References (Chapter 5—Extended)

Abbott, L. F., & Regehr, W. G. (2004). Synaptic computation. *Nature.* doi:10.1038/nature03010

Bargmann, C. I. (2012). Beyond the connectome: How neuromodulators shape neural circuits. *BioEssays.* doi:10.1002/bies.201100185

Clark, A. (2016). *Surfing uncertainty: Prediction, action, and the embodied mind.* Oxford University Press. https://www.goodreads.com/book/show/25823558

Damasio, A. R. (2018). *The strange order of things: Life, feeling, and the making of cultures.* Pantheon Books.

Fields, R. D. (2009). *The other brain: From dementia to schizophrenia, how new discoveries about the brain are revolutionizing medicine and science.* Simon & Schuster.

Friston, K. (2010). The free energy principle: A rough guide to the brain? *Nature Reviews Neuroscience.* doi:10.1038/nrn2787

Nedergaard, M. (2013). Neuroscience: Garbage truck of the brain. *Science*, 340(6140), 1529–1530. doi:10.1126/science.1240514

Companies

The following companies are actively working on technologies related to brain emulation, neural interfaces, consciousness research, and the broader goal of digital mind preservation.

Neuralink

Neuralink is a neurotechnology company founded by Elon Musk in 2016, focused on developing ultra-high-bandwidth brain–computer interfaces (BCIs). Their flagship device, the N1 implant, uses thousands of flexible electrode threads inserted into the cortex to read and write neural signals. In 2024, Neuralink began human clinical trials, enabling paralyzed patients to control computers with thought alone. The long-term vision includes memory augmentation and, ultimately, the ability to save and restore neural state—a direct step toward digital mind preservation.

Website: https://neuralink.com

Synchron

Synchron develops the Stentrode, a minimally invasive brain–computer interface delivered through the blood vessels rather than open-brain surgery. The device is placed in the motor cortex via the jugular vein and can record neural signals sufficient to control external devices. While currently focused on restoring motor function in ALS and paralysis patients, the platform represents a scalable path to chronic, high-bandwidth neural recording in everyday life.

Website: https://synchron.com

Cortical Labs

Cortical Labs (Melbourne, Australia) grows human neurons on silicon chips to create biological computing systems, branded as DishBrain. In 2022 they published landmark research in Neuron showing that cultured neurons can learn to play Pong in real time—demonstrating goal-directed behavior in vitro. The company is now developing CL1, a commercial biological intelligence platform. This work is directly relevant to understanding plasticity, learning, and the substrate requirements for mind emulation.

Website: https://corticallabs.com

Intel Neuromorphic Research Community (Loihi)

Intel's neuromorphic research program develops spiking neural network chips (Loihi, Loihi 2) that mimic how biological neurons communicate—using spikes rather than continuous values. These chips are highly energy-efficient and can run large-scale neural simulations orders of magnitude faster than conventional hardware. The Intel Neuromorphic Research Community (INRC) provides access to Loihi hardware for researchers worldwide. Neuromorphic hardware is considered a key enabling technology for real-time brain emulation at scale.

Website: https://intel.com/neuromorphic

MergeLab

MergeLab is a research-driven neurotechnology startup (co-founded by Sam Altman) that emerged from stealth in early 2026 with backing from OpenAI. Unlike electrode-based systems, Merge is pioneering a "molecular" and "acoustic" approach to BCIs. Their technology aims to use ultrasound to communicate with neurons—potentially enhanced by gene therapies that make specific brain cells visible to sound waves. This "soft merge" strategy seeks to bypass invasive surgery while achieving the high bandwidth necessary for a seamless interface between biological and artificial intelligence.

Website: https://merge.io

Reference

Berg, S. et al. (2025). Sexual dimorphism in the complete connectome of the Drosophila male central nervous system. *bioRxiv (preprint)*. doi:10.1101/2025.10.09.680999

Index

Page numbers in *italics* refer to figures.

For Product Safety Concerns and Information please contact our EU
representative GPSR@taylorandfrancis.com
Taylor & Francis Verlag GmbH, Kaufingerstraße 24, 80331 München, Germany

www.ingramcontent.com/pod-product-compliance
Lightning Source LLC
LaVergne TN
LVHW011934090926
847529LV00029B/219

* 9 7 8 1 0 4 1 3 4 8 1 5 3 *